What Hyenas Laughing At, Anyway?

ID0468689

Most Berkley Books are available at special quantity discounts for bulk purchases for sales promotions, premiums, fund-raising or educational use. Special books, or book excerpts, can also be created to fit specific needs.

For details, write to Special Markets: The Berkley Publishing Group, 200 Madison Avenue, New York, NY 10016.

Other Books by David Feldman

What Are Hyenas Laughing At, Anyway?

An Imponderables® Book

DAVID FELDMAN

ILLUSTRATED BY KASSIE SCHWAN

BERKLEY BOOKS, NEW YORK

WHAT *ARE* HYENAS LAUGHING AT, ANYWAY?

A Berkley Book/published by arrangement with
the author

PRINTING HISTORY
G. P. Putnam's Sons edition/October 1995
Berkley trade paperback edition/October 1996

All rights reserved.
Copyright © 1995 by David Feldman.
Illustrations © 1995 by Kassie Schwan.
Cover illustrations © 1995 by Lisa Goldrick.
Book design by Deborah Kerner.
This book may not be reproduced in whole or in part,
by mimeograph or any other means, without permission.
For information address: The Berkley Publishing Group,
200 Madison Avenue, New York, New York 10016.

The Putnam Berkley World Wide Web site address is http://www.berkley.com

ISBN 0-425-15451-3

BERKLEY®
Berkley Books are published by The Berkley Publishing Group,
200 Madison Avenue, New York, New York 10016.
BERKLEY and the "B" design
are trademarks belonging to Berkley Publishing Corporation.

PRINTED IN THE UNITED STATES OF AMERICA

10   9   8   7   6

For

UDAY IVATURY

and

LAURA TOLKOW

Contents

Preface

❧ Don't get us wrong. You can live a long, happy life if you don't ever wonder why mosquitoes like to bite some folks more than others. You aren't abnormal if you've never lost sleep over how convicts got into the license plate business. And we're confident that many bright people have never been distracted from their work by obsessing over why pharmacists work on raised platforms.

Indeed, we don't claim any moral superiority. We would guess that Mother Teresa has never lost a night's sleep wondering why men spit more than women.

But some of us can't help it. We see daily life as a never-ending series of conundrums that make no sense whatsoever. So think of this book as a literary self-help group for the curious.

And like all support groups, this isn't a one-person operation. Our readers send in the little mysteries of everyday life that drive them nuts—Imponderables, mysteries that can't be answered by standard reference books. We then contact experts to find the answers.

When we have trouble finding a satisfying answer to an Imponderable, we ask readers to help (we call these frustrating Imponderables "Frustable"). And when you have a bone to pick with our answers, we let you have a chance to state your case in the "Letters" section.

As a small token of our gratitude, if you're the first to submit an Imponderable we use in a book or provide the best solution to a new Frustable, we offer a grateful acknowledgment and complimentary copy of the volume with your contribution.

We're happy to announce that our support group is becoming interactive in two new ways. First, we are embarking on a scary project: to track down the mysteries of the opposite sex. As the last page of this book details, we welcome your contributions in this attempt to unravel the ultimate puzzle.

And second, we have taken Imponderability to cyberspace. If you have access to either Internet or Prodigy, we welcome your E-mail in lieu of "snail mail."

The last two pages of this book will tell you how you can reach us and join the fellowship. But as folks smitten with the plague ourselves, we know you're tensing up already, flooded with repressed memories of debilitating Imponderability. So for now, why not just enjoy the book and silently repeat: "I'm OK. I'm OK."

Imponderables

The Hyenas catch an episode of "The Jackals"

Why Are Hyenas Laughing?

❧ So, what *are* hyenas laughing at, anyway?

  A) At their prey before consuming them
  B) That Whoopi Goldberg was chosen to dub the voices of hyenas in *The Lion King*
    C) Jerry Lewis movies (French hyenas only)
    D) None of the above

Trick question. The correct answer is D. For as far as we know, humans are the only animals that laugh. And laughing is about the last thing on the minds of hyenas when they emit the extremely loud, high-pitched series of "hee-hee-hee's" that are called "giggles" by zoologists. We've heard tape recordings of these giggles, and we can only echo the sentiments of Peter Hathaway Capstick, who in *Outdoor Life* compared the sound to "a mad woman slowly being sawed in half without anaesthetic."

Although there are four surviving species of hyenas (brown, striped, spotted, and aardwolf), Carmi Penny, curator of mammals at the San Diego Zoo, says that with rare exceptions, only the spotted hyena giggles. Far from expressing pleasure or humor, hyenas display giggling behavior when threatened, chased, or attacked.

We spoke to research zoologist Laurence Frank, a member of the Berkeley Project, who is part of a rare research study of hyenas in captivity (spotted hyenas are found in the wild only in Africa, south of the Sahara). Frank informed us that hyenas are the Bobby McFerrin of carnivores, possessing one of the widest ranges of vocalizations of any terrestrial mammal (Hans Kruuk, in his landmark 1972 book, *The Spotted Hyena,* cataloged twelve distinct hyena sounds). Their loud whoop, which can be heard more than five kilometers away, serves as an eerie mating call by hyenas when walking alone (as Frank puts it, it's the hyena's way of saying, "I'm here, I want a girlfriend") and an unwanted wake-up call for any unfortunate humans who happen to be trying to sleep during what can only be described as a cacophonous all-night whoop-fest.

In the wild, hyenas giggling can be heard most often when they are attacked by lions or other hyenas, or when squabbling over the fruits of a kill (hyenas are predators and carnivores). When hyenas are bickering, the aggressor will occasionally emit the call, but Frank says that it's usually the victim—the giggle is a sign of defensiveness or distress, not aggression. As ironic as it sounds, Frank concludes: "A laughing hyena is not a happy hyena."

Submitted by Teresa Johnson of New York, New York.

☆n the Kellogg's Rice Krispies Cereal Box, Snap! Is Always Depicted as a Baker and Pop! as a Soldier. What Does Crackle! Do for a Living?

Funny. We've never been asked what Speedy does for a living (he hawks Alka-Seltzer), or how Mr. Peanut makes ends meet (he implores you to buy Planters products). So we hope that reader Sheila Ryan won't be disappointed to learn that as far as we can ascertain, Crackle's sole vocation is enticing you to buy the box of cereal on which he appears.

Rice Krispies was introduced in 1928, and its earliest advertising campaigns focused on the ruckus that the cereal makes when put in milk (if you want to know why, see *When Do Fish Sleep?*). Kellogg's chose "Snap! Crackle! Pop!" to describe the sounds. The three-word slogan first appeared on the front of the package in 1932.

But it wasn't until 1933 that the character Snap! appeared, on the box, solo, depicted as a tiny gnome. He wore then, as he does today, a baker's hat. Gnomes Crackle! and Pop! didn't join in the fun until the mid-1930s. Pop! donned military hats and Crackle!, although always seen adorned with a red or striped stocking cap, never wore a vocationally oriented uniform.

We spoke to our favorite Kellogg's source, Diane Dickey, a veritable Boswell of Crackle!, who told us that to her knowledge, the boys never changed these signature sartorial trademarks, except during World War II, when they posed "with guns, tanks, and ships that urged consumers to 'Save time, save fuel, save energy.' "

The hats of our heroes were important not only to differentiate the three of them, but to reinforce the Rice Krispies slogan, as a corporate history explains:

"According to one agency legend, the three gnomes didn't have their names until a creative layout artist extended lines from the cereal bowl so that the words Snap! Crackle! and Pop! landed on their hats—where they've been ever since.

"In 1949, Snap! Crackle! and Pop! changed drastically from gnomes with huge noses and ears and oversized hats, to more human creatures with boyish haircuts, proportional features, and smaller hats. They continued to evolve as fashions changed, appearing with longer or shorter hair, rounder eyes, and different costumes. Their hats have changed least."

Indeed. We're afraid that poor Crackle! is stuck with the identity of being the dude with the red hat, forever flanked by Snap! and Pop!. As Dickey wryly put it, "Crackle! is the classic middle child." But it's not as if we see Snap! baking Rice Krispies or Pop! defending Kellogg's from attacks by Cap'n Crunch.

Submitted by Sheila Ryan of Nelson, British Columbia

Why Do Pharmacists Stand on Raised Platforms Behind High Counters in [the Back of] Most Drugstores?

✃ We were tempted to say that if *you* were working with drugs all day, you'd be high, too. But then we resisted.

Many pharmacists were willing to help us explain why pharmacists stand on platforms now, but we weren't able to get a fix on earlier practice until we heard from Greg Higby, director of the American Institute of the History of Pharmacy at the University of Wisconsin. Higby brings us up to speed on the history of the drugstore platform until World War II.

Before about 1870, prescription compounding areas were by necessity located in the front of the store, near the window—artificial illumination couldn't provide sufficient light for the pharmacist to work effectively. Soda fountains became a craze after 1870, and most drugstores found them to be important profit centers. These fountains, along with better artificial lighting, pushed prescription areas to the back of the store, which hastened other changes. According to Higby:

> "From the 1870s through the 1930s, prescription departments were commonly hidden behind a screen or wall from public view. The goods in the stores were sold by clerks from cabinets (no self service).
>
> "Self-service was introduced gradually after 1920. This encouraged pharmacists to open up their prescription departments a bit, sometimes with just a window or viewing hole, so that they could keep an eye on their stock.
>
> "After 1940, many pharmacies remodeled and opened up their Rx departments more. Not only did they want to watch their stock, but they also wanted customers to see them in the back (as evidence of the store's professional owner). Prescription volume increased greatly after 1945, so pharmacists were in the back filling prescriptions more and more; therefore, they could not police the floor as well."

As Higby implies, typically many pharmacists were also the managers of their stores. According to RPh Marsha Holloman, of the American Pharmaceutical Association, one of the main reasons for the high platform was security:

> "Traditionally, the pharmacy portion of the drugstore was located in the rear. The pharmacist stood on a raised platform in order to have an unobstructed view of the entire store [handy for spotting shoplifters]. The high prescription counters discouraged patients and customers from entering the area of the drugstore where prescription medications and poisons were kept. The high counters also made it difficult for would-be robbers to gain access to the pharmacy."

But platforms have been popular with pharmacists for a second reason: comfort. RPh Ron Cohen, of the Philadelphia Pharmacy, told *Imponderables* that after an eight- to twelve-hour shift, he appre-

ᗪavid ᖴeldman

ciates the cushiony feel of a wooden platform rather than the cold, hard concrete floor. As Holloman puts it,

> "A raised platform with a certain amount of give usually means the difference between a healthy, happy pharmacist and a lame, grouchy one!"

Jan Razek, of drugstore chain Revco, points out that a third advantage of a raised counter is greater recognition and prominence for the pharmacist, who is not only located far from the entrance to the store, but would be otherwise visually obscured by aisles of bandages, analgesics, and foot deodorizers.

But all of the pharmacists we spoke to said that the raised platform is increasingly going the way of the drugstore soda fountain. Razek reports that many chains are eliminating the high counters because "customers feel they are being talked down to." Accelerating the demise of the high counter is the increasing interaction among customers and pharmacists. Many pharmacies now feature areas where pharmacists can meet with patrons privately. With the deterioration, for many, of the family doctor-patient relationship, pharmacists have increasingly become the major source for information about medications. As Razek puts it,

> "The traditional view of the pharmacist ensconced in the pharmacy behind a high counter and peering down from a raised platform is fast disappearing. I hope that the new view of the pharmacist is of the concerned medication expert who has permanently emerged from behind the pharmacy counter to talk with and educate patients on the proper management of their therapeutic regimens."

All well and good. But do we want to be counseled by a lame, grouchy, platformless pharmacist?

Submitted by Bruce W. Miller of Riverside, Connecticut. Thanks also to David E. Corley of Topeka, Kansas; Todd Lesko of Laguna Niguel, California; and Edward B. Litherland of Rock Island, Illinois.

Why Is Tuna the Only Variety of Cat Food That Doesn't Come in a Pull-Tab Can?

☞ We admire persistence in our readers. Steve Thompson, a long-time contributor to *Imponderables*, wrote the following several years ago:

> "When I send lists of Imponderables to you, I never ask my wife for suggestions, but she just came up with an *excellent* one. Tuna cat food has to be opened with a can opener. This is true with every brand of cat food. Tuna for human consumption comes in pull-tab cans, so why not tuna for cats? She also wonders what part of the tuna is in cat food, since it is so much darker in color than tuna for humans.
>
> "This should *definitely* be in your next book, considering how many cat owners there are."

We're not sure that every cat owner is waiting on tenterhooks for the answer to this Imponderable, but considering the number of dog Imponderables, we feel we owe owners of felines a sop (especially if each buys a copy or two of this book!).

Occasionally, Steve would issue updates on this crisis:

> "My wife says that 'liver-and-tuna' and 'kidney-and-tuna' cat food comes in pull-tab cans, but just plain 'tuna' never does. The brands she knows for certain are: Alpo; Friskies; 9-Lives; Petuna; Ralphs; Springfield; Vons; and Whiskas."

And when Steve's helpful information didn't get him into the last book, he could even get a little testy:

ᨀ David Feldman

"Since my question about tuna cat food never being available in pull-tab cans is not in the new book, I'm sure you're still doing highly ambitious research into the matter, and it will be discussed in next year's book."

OK, Steve. It's right here! And Peggy's observations are correct: After contacting many different cat food manufacturers, we couldn't find one that sells "plain" tuna with a pull-tab can.

"Why?" we asked. Typical was the response of Judy Lederich, of Friskies PetCare Company's office of consumer affairs:

"We use two different types of cans for Friskies canned cat food. Each type comes from a different can supplier and source. The cans for the tuna flavor are made of steel, and this flavor is manufactured and canned in Thailand. They do not have a pull tab. The cans for all other flavors are made of aluminum; these other flavors are manufactured and canned locally. The aluminum cans have a pull-tab. Both are recyclable.

"The tuna flavor is made in Thailand because of the availability of high-quality tuna in that part of the world. Packing the tuna in Thailand, immediately after it is caught, makes a higher-quality product than freezing the tuna and shipping it to the United States for packing. Cats have a keen sense of taste and smell, and they do notice the difference...."

Part of the price paid by cat food companies for the cheaper sources of tuna overseas is the relative primitiveness of available canning facilities. For example, food giant Heinz owns both Star-Kist and 9-Lives. Heinz utilizes tuna-canning facilities in such far-flung localities as American Samoa and Ghana. In these plants, the light meat of the tuna would be used for Star-Kist and the red meat for 9-Lives. According to Debbie Bolding, communications manager for Star-Kist, American consumers disdain the red meat of tuna, largely because they find the dark meat unsightly, but cats prefer it. But many of their canning facilities overseas are not fitted for manufacturing pull-tab cans.

So, Steve and Peggy, while you may be deprived of the convenience of pull-tabs for your tuna cat food, rest assured that human consumers of tuna from the same plants must also resort to the dreaded can opener.

Submitted by Steve and Peggy Thompson of La Crescenta, California. Thanks also to Laurie Pollack of Upper Darby, Pennsylvania; Adam Goldman of Sharon, Massachusetts; and Paul Swinford of Cincinnati, Ohio.

Why Do Many Guitar Players Leave a Long Bit of String Hanging Off in the Air at the Tuning End of the Guitar?

Guitar strings are considerably longer than needed, largely to compensate for the varying lengths of different instruments. Rock stars hire roadies to take care of mundane activities such as clipping off excess string with wire cutters before the guitarist needs to play. Less successful pros and home players usually cut the strings themselves, usually with wire clippers.

Still, the picture of the guitar soloist with face contorted behind a mass of labyrinthine string ends (the tuning end of the guitar is known as the "headstock") is enough of a cliché to lead us to the inevitable: "Why?" We received a charming letter from Mark W. Blythe, a guitar technician at renowned Fender Musical Instruments. Blythe offered the five theories below. We've supplemented his quotes with our correspondence with guitarists on both the Internet guitarists' Usenet group (rec.music.guitars) and Prodigy's music/musicians' board:

1. *"The roadie did not have time to clip the excess string off the machine before the guitarist needed the instrument."*

2. *"The roadie [or guitarist] lost his wire clippers."*

3. *"Some musicians are just lazy."*

Guitarist Joshua Bardwell says that if you can't find a wire cutter, then the safest way to cut the wire is to do the "bend-back-and-forth-'til-it-breaks method," the ritual by which most of us break paper clips.

4. *"The excess string is used in emergency string repair situations. You can take the string off and retie the ball end to the end of the string. The extra amount of string is then used to compensate for the amount of string that was lost when it was broken."*

Amateur guitarist Rich Beerman not only saves himself from "emergencies" but saves money by using this method. When he breaks a string, he unlocks it from the tremolo, throws out the part of the string connected to the tremolo, and then takes the part attached to the tuner on the headstock and pulls it toward the tremolo. "Once the end of the string is back at the tremolo, you lock it back in place."

5. *"Some musicians are eccentric and believe the removal of the extra string will result in lost tone."*

Paul Bagley, who performs in several different bands, wrote us:

> "I used to leave my strings at full length until a pro musician friend convinced me to run a simple test. After the strings are installed and at proper pitch, there was no difference in tone between the cut and uncut strings. Since then I've cut them off pretty close to the tuning machine."

Echoing this sentiment is guitarist Stephen Teter, who points out one disadvantage of extra-long strings:

> "If you are recording, the hanging strings can be picked up slapping against each other, bleeding into the recording (usually in a 'silent' spot)."

David Feldman

Our cyberspace sources added three more possible explanations for the case of the dangling string:

6. *Sometimes the "extra" string actually is a string.* UK musician Jonathan Egre points out that some guitarists place string around the headstock in order to be able to hang the guitar on a peg in the wall, and in the case of some thrifty types, as a substitute for a proper guitar strap.

7. *The Ouch Theory.* Player Steve Cowell writes: "The guitarist may be tired of poking the ends of fingers on short cut-off wires—you bleed like a stuck pig."

8. *The Cool Theory.* Guitarist Tim Shelfer agrees: "There's a lot of prestige in loose wire on your headstock, for only who knows why." "The Rickmeister," Rick Nedderman, knows why:

> "I think it's some sort of artistic statement or trade secret that we uninitiated, uncool dweebs just haven't been made privy to. If you've seen photos of players with a tangle of excess strings at the headstock, it's obvious from the intense facial expression (you know the one: eyes closed, eyebrows lifted way up) that it makes one a much more creative player. After all, untangling your left hand (or right) from that mess after you just played the most awesome open E power chord of your entire life takes a lot of creative thinking."

Submitted by Michael Colvin of Lawrence, Kansas.

Why Are Autopsies Performed on Criminals Who Have Just Been Executed?

A convicted murderer is brought into a chamber. He is strapped to an electric chair. The executioner flips the switch. The prisoner dies.

One wouldn't think that Quincy would be required to diagnose the cause of death. Yet, as far as we know, every state that has capital punishment requires an autopsy to be performed on the executed prisoner. In discussing this strange requirement with many forensics practitioners and medical examiners, three themes recurred:

1. Ascertaining the cause of death can still be contested, even if it seems obvious. For legal reasons, states find it prudent to protect themselves. Michael Graham, Chief Medical Examiner of St. Louis, Missouri, explains:

> "Because execution is the most extreme punishment possible for a crime, it is necessary to establish the cause of death to the fullest extent of reasonable certainty. The basis for giving an opinion about the cause of death should be able to withstand challenge such as, 'He really didn't die from the injection but was killed in some other manner beforehand.' "

2. An autopsy documents the criminal's pre-execution condition. Says Graham:

> "An autopsy will reveal the presence or absence of any pre-existing diseases, injuries or potential toxic substances (alcohol, drugs, poisons). An autopsy would help to support or refute any allegations that the criminal experienced physical abuse or was under the influence of toxicants prior to the execution."

Dr. Bill Hamilton, who has performed autopsies on executed prisoners in Gainesville, Florida, recalls that when the body of the first prisoner executed in Florida under the latest capital punishment law was shipped to California for burial, a cemetery official found what he thought to be signs of torture and physical abuse on the remains. Eventually, the body was exhumed and the "abuse" turned out to be electrical burns associated with electrocutions. Routine autopsies would forestall such accusations, or at least confirm or rebut them.

<del>ᴏᴎᴑ</del>   𝔇avid 𝔽eldman

3. But perhaps the most common reason why autopsies are performed on most executed prisoners, according to Dr. Lowell Levine of the New York State Police Forensics Science Unit, is more mundane. Most states have laws specifying that *any* person who dies in custody of prison systems must be autopsied. In this litigious age, the last thing state penal systems need are lawsuits or investigative journalists hounding them years after an execution.

Submitted by Nelson T. Sparks of Louisa, Kentucky.

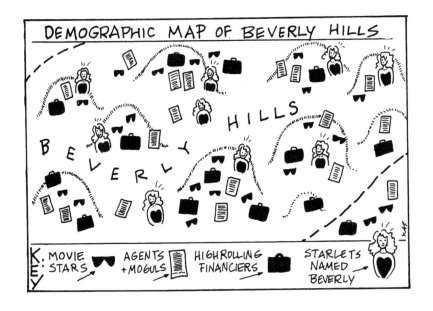

DEMOGRAPHIC MAP OF BEVERLY HILLS

BEVERLY HILLS

KEY: MOVIE STARS — AGENTS + MOGULS — HIGH ROLLING FINANCIERS — STARLETS NAMED BEVERLY

Who or Where Was the Beverly Referred to in "Beverly Hills"?

Less than one hundred years before Aaron Spelling decided to immortalize the ZIP code 90210, the area now known as Beverly Hills had a decidedly less glamorous name: El Rancho de las Aguas. And the town's beginnings were humble as well: It was part of an old Spanish land grant.

But Burton E. Green had loftier ideas. He founded the town, dubbed it "Beverly Hills" in 1906, and proceeded to subdivide the land for residential abodes. Eight years later, the city was incorporated. According to Fred Cunningham, executive director of public affairs and information for the city of Beverly Hills, Green borrowed the name "Beverly" from Beverly Farms, the Massachusetts retreat of soon-to-be-President Howard Taft. The "Hills" was an obvious allusion to the rolling topography of the area.

David Feldman

Don't assume that any geographical place named "Beverly" is necessarily honoring a particular paragon of female pulchritude: "Beverly" is derived from a Middle English word that means "beaver."

Submitted by David Altom of Hutchinson, Kansas.

Modern Architecture vs. Second-Story Work...

Why Do Buildings Have Ledges?

✎ When researching this Imponderable, we followed our usual course of looking at standard reference books. Although *we* didn't know the answer to the question, we assumed that any good reference book on architecture would have an answer. And if we found an answer, we'd give up our attempt to answer this mystery.

But all we found were vague definitions. It didn't matter whether we consulted *Webster's* or the *Architectural and Building Trades Dictionary*—about all we could glean was that a ledge was defined in architecture as "any shelflike projection from a wall."

Great. We knew *that* much.

We went wrong in assuming that ledges must have a practical function, for it seems that they usually do not. We thought perhaps that they served as a structural companion to windowsills, but ledges serve no structural role in maintaining the integrity of the sill or the building as a whole. Norman Cox, a partner with Franke, Gottesgen, Cox Architects, told *Imponderables* that at least sills do serve an important function: to direct water away from the window opening and to allow the water to drip free of the wall, thereby protecting the wall from staining and other damage.

Cox added that sometimes ledges may align with the windowsills of a building:

> "This would usually be the result of an aesthetic decision, although there might be a constructional advantage to combining the string course [a horizontal molding, usually of brick or stone, set in the wall of a building] and the windowsill."

Cox argues that the ledges in old buildings were an attempt to follow classical conceptions of composition, the orders of architecture, the stuff that we were taught about architecture in high school history classes. Remember those Doric and Corinthian columns you were tested on in school? They all featured entablatures, horizontal superstructures that were supported by the columns.

The purpose of the entablatures was to balance visually the strong vertical sweep of the columns. Similarly, ledges on multistoried buildings provide a strong horizontal line, according to Vancouver architect Maura Gatensby:

> "Ledges can be used to make the mass of the building appear less imposing. Sometimes the horizontal line is reinforced by a change of material or colour, but mostly the ledge effect comes from the strong shadow line it creates."

Of course, modern architects often deliberately try to make their skyscrapers look and feel imposing. Windows in many office buildings often no longer open. And ledges have disappeared from most. When architects choose to cast away the orders of architecture, they usually prefer to emphasize the vertical. No ledge is going to interrupt the flow of their continuous vertical lines!

Our most intriguing response to this Imponderable came from

an architect who will remain nameless to protect his reputation. He wondered if the real purpose of ledges wasn't to keep pigeon droppings off (or away from) the building facade. One problem with this theory: Although the ledge may solve one problem, it creates another—pigeon droppings on the darn ledge.

Submitted by Nelson T. Sparks of Louisa, Kentucky.

Why Is Leather So Expensive?

❧ Our correspondents wondered why the skin of a cow is so expensive when hamburger is so cheap. A pair of simple leather athletic shoes might set you back $50 to $75; a bomber jacket, $200 to $500; a leather couch, $1,000 up to the stratosphere.

Charlie Myers, of the Leather Industries of America, is quick to say: "Hey, don't look at us." And he has a point. The wholesale price of leather is cheaper, much cheaper, than you probably expect. Raw cattle hide fetches about ninety cents per pound as this is being written, and after being shipped overseas for tanning, comes back fully processed, costing approximately $2 per foot for the standard grades used in most leather jackets and low-end shoes.

> "First-class leather today [the type used in Timberland Shoes or the best car interiors] sells for about $3.00 per foot. There are perhaps 2 to $2\frac{1}{2}$ feet of leather in a pair of shoes. If you pay $130 for a pair of waterproof hiking shoes, what else besides the $6 to $7.50 for the leather goes into the cost?

"Put another way, in 1993 a pair of white leather athletic shoes, made in China, entered U.S. Customs and paid duty on $7.79 per pair. That was the 'first cost' of those shoes. My kids would go to the mall on Saturday and pay $55 for those shoes that cost $7.79 when they entered this country. What in the heck is going on here?"

As you might guess, shoe industry types aren't too excited about explaining exactly "what the heck is going on here?" According to Myers's statistics, nearly 90 percent of the shoes produced in the U.S. are imported, mostly from the Far East. We can't help but think that shoe costs are driven up by "marketing expenses," such as millions for Shaquille O'Neal and Deion Sanders, and soft-sell image advertisements, along with the necessary merchandising and design costs.

John J. Moynihan, of the Shoe Trades Publishing Company, was frank enough to admit that the price of leather goods is largely dependent upon market forces:

"The production of a consumer leathergood, from the flaying of the animal to the manufacture of the product, is a very time-consuming, labor-intensive process. Maybe the question is: Why is time and labor so expensive?

"Moreover, leather is 'expensive' because there is [constant] demand for it. The supply of the raw material is fixed. No one kills a cow for its hide. There is a 'shortage' of leather-making material, pushing up the price of the raw material. The demand for leather is inelastic. Hence price increases do not reduce demand by a similar percentage amount.

"The real Imponderable is not why leather is so expensive but why are neckties so expensive?"

Nice try, John, but we'll get to *that* Imponderable another time.

Because leather is a by-product of the meat industry, Glenda Karrenbrock, of Tandy Leather Company, offered a unique solution to the leather cost crisis:

"As the market for meat declines, in this new diet-conscious age, the ranchers cut back their production. When this happens, there are fewer hides produced and the market price goes up.

". . . If we are going to ever see the leather market fall . . . we are going to have to eat more beef!"

So vegetarians are to blame for the high cost of leather!

Submitted by Alice Cammon of Chicago, Illinois. Thanks also to William Janna of Memphis, Tennessee, and J. H. Yim of Berkeley, California.

Why Do Parrots Often Bob Their Heads Up and Down, Especially When Spoken To?

☞ We always assumed that when parrots bobbed up and down, they were nodding their approval at the bon mots we were uttering. Alas, although parrots are extremely intelligent, their command of English isn't *that* strong.

Martha Fischer, of the Cornell Lab of Ornithology, told *Imponderables* that the most common reasons for head bobbing among most birds are to locate sound and to see objects better. But parrots, alas, are another breed.

We heard from Todd Lee Etzel, national coordinator of the Society of Parrot Breeders and Exhibitors, and he revealed his two, pardon the expression, pet theories about this Imponderable. Etzel believes that though the parrots might have been excited by our speaking to them, it wasn't because of the intellectual content therein:

"Courtship for parrots is a complicated series of vocal and visual displays. Many species utilize head bobbing in unison to help solidify the pair bond. When we speak to a pet parrot that is properly socialized as a pet, the head bobbing is often a signal of the bird's excitement at the attention and even a signal for a desire to begin courtship display with a potential 'mate.'

"Another theory to explain head bobbing begins with the birth of the parrot. Parrots regurgitate food for their offspring and grab the babies' beak with theirs, feeding with a bobbing motion as they bring up food from their crop to feed the baby. Older babies that have been weaned will still beg to be fed by grabbing a finger and undulating the head in 'baby posture.'

"Some behaviorists believe that is the source for head bobbing behavior. I feel the courtship response is more appropriate as the posture of most birds when head bobbing is not a 'baby posture' (the head being held back at a sharp angle with the beak in an appropriate position for feeding).

"So my answer would be: The parrot wants a date."

What could be sexier than head bobbing, after all? Why bother bobbing for apples when you can bob for babes?

Submitted by Donna Yavelak of Norcross, Virginia.

Why Do Pilots Turn Off the Interior Lights Before Taking Off?

☞ "If you're talking about the lights going out for any period of time," replied one pilot, "that's when the crew is having a party in the cockpit."

Thanks, we didn't need that.

There are actually two moments when the lights are killed in the cabin. The first is merely a flicker. John Payton, an airline electrician, explains:

"While the craft is sitting at the gate, it is hooked up to an auxiliary power unit, which provides power for cabin lighting and ventilation. When the engines are running, they switch over to power generated by the engines and disconnect this auxiliary unit."

But if you are referring to the practice of main cabin lights being extinguished during takeoff, it has nothing to do with safety or technical problems. The flight attendants turn out the lights. United Airlines captain Mike Lauria claims that the lights-out custom is motivated by passengers' desire to better see the lights *outside* the plane on takeoff (pilots do control the emergency lights located on the floor).

Note that on landing, even at night, interior lights are usually illuminated. Why? Passengers are usually concerned with gathering up their personal effects. And flight attendants don't want the dubious pleasure of waking up slumbering passengers.

Submitted by Bill Van Koevering of Maple Grove, Minnesota.

Pachyderm Habitat
(formerly Elephant House)

DO NOT:
• Feed
• Lend Any
  Audio
  Tapes

Why Do Elephants in Zoos Rock From Side to Side While Otherwise Standing Still? Do They Exhibit the Same Behavior in the Wild?

☙ Veterinarian Myron Hinrichs, of Hasti Friends of the Elephant, issued a warning to us: "One can never be certain that zoo behavior is natural behavior, because it can come from boredom." And none of the other sources we contacted disagrees. Whether or not we are anthropomorphizing when we use "boredom" to describe the reaction of elephants in zoos, pachyderms and most other animals find some relief in enriching their environment by performing these types of rituals.

Still, this kind of rocking does serve a more important purpose. Ed Hansen, executive director of the American Association of Zoo Keepers, notes that this kind of rocking is sometimes called "weaving," and can aid the normal digestive process of all monogastric (one-stomach) animals.

Hansen adds that at some point in their lives, most nonwild elephants are chained for one reason or another. Some elephants learn to manipulate the chains by swinging them back and forth and continue the behavior even when off chains.

By all accounts, elephants do rock in place in the wild. In her book *Elephant Memories*, Cynthia Moss calls this motion "the characteristic elephant gesture of indecision."

Submitted by Tom and Marcia Bova of Rochester, New York.

Why Do Umpires Turn Around to Sweep Off Home Plate?

Any baseball fan has noticed that umpires perform a strange ritual when brushing off home plate. While they could clean off the dirt by simply bending straight down, umpires invariably walk around the plate and face the fans before accomplishing the humble task.

It wasn't always so. We spoke to Dr. Larry R. Gerlach, professor of history at the University of Utah, who is the most knowledgeable human in the universe on the history of umpiring. Gerlach reports that before the turn of the century, umpires dusted off the plate with a long, "regular" broom, which was kept leaning against the backstop or in the dugout. It wasn't until the twentieth century that the whisk broom made its first appearance, and it became commonplace by World War I.

Between world wars, umpires were self-taught: Some umpires turned to brush off the plate; others stood their ground. Formal umpiring schools became the recognized training grounds for professional baseball just after World War II, and these schools were responsible for the standardization of umpire procedures. According to Gerlach, these schools all taught umps to turn around—and for the last fifty years, this practice has been *de rigueur*. The tradition persists even though there is no specific rule or regulation covering where the umpire should stand to perform his cleaning job.

Jim Evans, major league umpire for the past twenty-three years and owner of the Jim Evans Academy of Professional Umpiring (one of the three major professional umpiring schools), reports that all schools teach fledgling umps to turn around when dusting the plate:

> "It doesn't really matter whether they [umpiring students] know the reason, as long as they have the proper technique and mechanics."

Maybe it isn't important for students to know why they turn around before dusting off the plate, but it is crucial to us, right? Why the "wasted effort"? To answer this daunting Imponderable, we've assembled an All-Star panel of our own, experts on the recondite field of umpiring. They advanced five different theories. In roughly descending order of emphasis, they are:

1. *Accentuate the Positive.*

Nearly every expert we consulted mentioned that as a sign of courtesy and respect for the fans, the umpire should present his "better" side. As retired umpire Carl Lewton learned in umpire school forty-five years ago, "Don't show your butt to the stands."

Indeed, minor league umpire (and head linesman in the National Football League) Dale Williams admits that during a long game on a hot day, he occasionally steps up quickly and wipes the plate with his backside to the stands. But so ingrained is the custom that he feels uncomfortable about it. Of course, any umpire working a game in a ballpark with outfield bleachers is exposing his rear end to the farsighted gawkers in the outfield bleachers, anyway.

2. *Eliminate the Negative.*

We were festooned with stories of umpires splitting their pants (with what we've seen of many umpires' ever-burgeoning physiques, we understand how *that* happens). After speaking to umpires of yore, Gerlach reports that many of the pre–World War II umpires claimed that their most embarrassing moment in baseball was when they ripped their pants. The seam-distress was responsible, in some cases, for their turning around when brushing the plate.

Joe Reed, a retired umpire, informed *Imponderables* that many umps wear dark underwear to minimize the embarrassment if their pants rip, "just in case." But the turning was a spontaneous gesture after the fact. We couldn't find a single anecdote about a pants-splitting occurring *while* brushing off the plate. Several of our sources, such as former umpire Tom Hammill, now editor of *Referee* magazine, mentioned that most rips occur while the umpire is calling balls and strikes in the crouched position.

3. *Latch on to the Affirmative.*

Two of our experts registered strong dissents from the majority. Both Lance Deckinger, of the National Baseball Congress, and Jerry Aronow, a former minor league umpire, assert that there is a more important reason for umpires to turn: safety. Aronow, who graduated from Harry Wendelstedt's umpiring school, distinctly remembers being taught that it is prudent never to have your head exposed to an errant throw from a pitcher or fielder.

Come to think of it, if pitchers intentionally bean opposition batters, why not call an open season on umpires? Better to be hit on your rear than your cranium, argue these two.

Most of our other sources discounted this theory, claiming that no umpire who values his body would turn to dust the plate without making sure that all the players knew there was a time-out. Gerlach mentions that no pitcher would ever fling the ball unless an opposing player was in the batter's box.

4. *Don't Mess With Mr. In-Between.*

Hammill notes that most of the time, there is a big obstacle to sweeping the plate while facing the pitcher—the catcher: "As a practical matter, you *have* to go around anyway."

So even if turning around usually ends up being more convenient to the umpire, occasionally you'll see a lackadaisical ump seek out a method considerably less labor-intensive. Joe Reed notes that while umpires used to wear spikes, like the players, many now wear shoes with rubber-ripple soles. Occasionally, you'll see an umpire, while still facing the pitcher, simply scrape the plate with his shoe. Reed says this swipe can eliminate an isolated smudge of dirt. The big advantage of this procedure is its quickness, which can obviate the need to call a time-out.

5. *The Real Reason Umpires Turn Around Is to Generate Interesting Stories to Help Authors Spice Up Their Books.*

Actually, none of our reputable sources would venture this theory for us, so we advance it ourselves as a pitiful excuse to share a few wonderful anecdotes that occurred during home plate "brush-offs." Actually, several umpires conceded that excessive plate cleaning is often an excuse for the umpire to say something to a player, usually the catcher. Reed mentioned that the most common instance for the *tête-à-tête* is when the catcher is griping excessively about balls-and-strikes calls. The umpire will walk in front of the plate, face the catcher, and while dusting it off, say something like: "Listen, I'm going to ump and you're going to catch. Got that?"

Jerry Aronow relates one such story. He was umpiring a high-school game when first baseman and hitting star John Elway (yes, the future NFL quarterback) was at bat. Jerry dusted the plate but left some dirt on the black area around the outside of the plate.

> Elway said: "Mr. Aronow, why don't you get the outside of the plate?"
>
> Aronow replied: "Because *you* need everything you can get."

We wonder if Aronow would repeat that statement today, at least if he weren't wearing protective gear.

When Jim Evans first hit the major leagues in 1971, he was, at twenty-three, the youngest umpire ever. One day he was behind the plate with veteran Tiger catcher Bill Freehan. At banquets, Jim Evans tells this story, which may or may not be apocryphal:

> "Bill was giving me a lot of guff. I asked my crew chief, Hank Soar, what to do about it and Hank said, 'Next time he holds a pitch on you, walk around, dust off the plate, look him in the eye and tell him if he holds another pitch, you're gonna bite his head off and he's gone.' ["Holding a pitch" is the practice of catchers keeping the ball in the mitt at the spot where the ball was caught to let the ump and the fans know that they dis-

approve of the call. Umpires consider holding the pitch to be a deliberate attempt to show them up.]

"Well, Freehan holds another pitch, so I thought I'd try what Hank said. I went around to dust off the plate. Now, Freehan was a former All-American at Michigan, about 6′4″ and 230 pounds. I said, while looking him in the face, 'Mr. Freehan, if you hold another pitch on me, I'm gonna bite your head off.'

"Freehan said: 'Mr. Evans, let me tell you something. If you bit my head off, you'd have more brains in your stomach than you do in your head.' "

Occasionally, the dialogue gets a little spicier than that. In his best-selling book, *Behind the Mask, My Double Life in Baseball,* umpire Dave Pallone recounts the following story about his training at the Umpire Development School (slightly modified by me for more delicate sensibilities), which summarizes well the sentiments of most of our experts:

"The Umpire Development Program was so thorough, they even worked us on the correct technique for brushing off home plate. They said, 'Keep your a**es down. An a** in the air is a stupid a**.' And they took it a step further. They pointed out: 'Always face the crowd when you brush off the plate. Never aim your a** at the fans.' I thought that made sense, too. 'Yeah,' one of us joked, 'it's better to aim your a** at pitchers. They think umpires are a**holes anyway.' "

Submitted by Stephen Murphy of Clayton, North Carolina.

Why Is Gold Bullion Made in the Shape of Bricks?

❧ Of course, gold comes in other forms, including ingots and bars. And gold coins have been renowned for their beauty as well as their expense in many nations. But the shape has endured: Gold bricks were cast at least as far back as Egypt, 3100 B.C., so there must be some reason for the longevity of the shape.

Think about who owns these gold bricks: governments and rich people. Many governments all over the world hoard gold. Fort Knox, for example, stores a mere 147.3 million ounces of gold bricks, according to U.S. Mint spokesperson Mike White. Rich folks are too busy making more money to sit and admire their treasure. You won't find gold bullion sitting on the mantelpiece in their mansions. Gold bricks tend to be kept in the sterile environment of bank vaults.

So for these two types of clientele, the shape of gold is more of a practical than aesthetic concern, as John H. Lutley, president of the Gold Institute, a worldwide association of suppliers of gold and gold products, makes clear:

"The rectangular shape makes these bars easy to handle and they stock compactly in the bank vaults around the world where they are mostly stored."

Bank (or any other) vaults are expensive to construct. Space is at a premium. Gold circles wouldn't stack easily and would waste space. Gold squares wouldn't be as easy to carry (they would be too squat to handle comfortably). Indeed, European ingots are tapered in order to make them more manageable than our rectangles.

Gold is so dense that carrying even relatively small bricks becomes a logistical problem (although there is no single standard, a typical gold brick measures 260 mm × 60 mm × 40 mm and weighs 27 pounds). Gold bricks are usually moved by hand, for they can't be stored on flats and moved by small forklifts—the weight of the bars would crush the flats. Even when gold is moved in armored cars, Lutley reports, the bricks must be stacked only one deep to prevent breaking the axle of the truck.

The density of gold is so high that the bricks are rarely moved. When ownership of gold is changed, most commonly the bars themselves are simply relabeled and kept in whatever storage facility the previous owner had used. It is far easier to transfer a few pieces of paper than tons of gold, even in "practical" brick form.

Submitted by a caller on the Mike Pintek Show on KDKA-AM, Pittsburgh, Pennsylvania.

Why Is Chianti Bottled in Straw-Covered Containers?

At least as far back as the thirteenth century, the red wine produced in the Chianti Mountains of the Tuscany region of Italy was sold in *fiaschi*, the round, chubby-bottomed glass bottles that traditionally have been covered with straw. From tax documents still extant, we know that millions of gallons of Chianti were shipped to Florence in 1298 alone.

Probably because the biggest industry of the Chianti region was wine production, Tuscany was a center of glassblowing as well. Indeed, a Florentine, Salvino D'Armato, who died in 1315, invented spectacles. The *fiaschi* were fine vessels for holding wine, but they presented a problem.

Because of their bulbous bottoms, *fiaschi* don't stack well, and the winegrowers didn't create special boxes to carry them. So an extremely labor-intensive solution was conceived to reconcile the special needs of Chianti. Thomas B. Busey, chief of the wine and beer branch of the Bureau of Alcohol, Tobacco and Firearms, explains:

> "The use of rounded straw-covered containers for chianti began . . . at a time when there were glassblowers to make sufficient rounded bottles and labor was plentiful to weave straw bottle covers. Generally, chianti was intended for the local market and was considered an ordinary red table wine.
>
> Before modern roads and means of transportation, the straw cover served a very useful purpose in protecting the fragile bottle when transported over rocky roads in animal-drawn carts."

Derek Holstein, winemaker at Guernoc Winery Estates Vineyard, told *Imponderables* that the fiber of choice for covering Chianti bottles was raffia, a palm tree from Madagascar. Raffia was strong enough not only to protect the bottles when jostled against each other, but to string several bottles together so that an improvised "six-pack" could be carried by one person.

Almost from inception, Chianti has been the Rodney Dangerfield of red wine. Although fine Chianti has always been produced, the sheer fecundity of the region's fields has led to a profusion of mediocre wine. And unscrupulous merchants have been known to export inferior product from other Italian regions bottled in the trademarked straw-covered flagon. The straw-covered vessels became emblematic of Chianti's image problems.

In the 1950s, empty Chianti bottles were often converted into lamps or used as candleholders. Although this fad raised the sales of Chianti temporarily, it also lent Chianti an unwanted downscale image. Combined with the sophisticated bottling techniques now available in Italy, the straw started gradually disappearing from Chianti bottles in the middle of this century. According to Lucio Caputo, of the Italian Wine & Food Institute, most Chianti is now bottled in "regular" wine bottles, usually in a standard claret shape known as "bordolese."

Most high-quality Chianti is bottle-aged. Busey says that straw presents a practical problem for vintners: "A round-shaped bottle does not stack well and straw tends to rot in damp wine cellars." And considering that most bottles are no longer sent to market in horse-drawn wagons, the only need for protective straw is to preserve nostalgia.

Submitted by Bert Garwood of Grand Forks, North Dakota.

Why Is the U.S. Flag Painted Backward on Aircraft and Space Shuttles?

❧ Normally, of course, the stars are located on the upper-left portion of the American flag. But it is not uncommon to see aircraft where the stars (also known as the *canton*, the upper corner closest to the staff) are on the upper right.

Why are airplanes different? The National Flag Foundation explains:

> "Proper display of the flag in motion emanates from a single principle. The flag always 'flies forward.' That is, the canton (stars) on the flag is oriented towards the front of the moving object as though it were being carried on a staff and moving in a forward direction."

The custom is to display the American flags on *both* sides of a plane, usually on the vertical stabilizer in the back of the aircraft. Thus, the flag will fly "backward" half of the time. If you happen to be looking at the left side of the aircraft (i.e., the left side from the passengers' point of view), the stars will be on the left (or normal position); if you walk around to the right side of the aircraft, the canton will be on your right.

Similarly, the U.S. Air Force requires that "The bars of the flag will appear to be trailing at all times." NASA space shuttles conform to the American Standards for Display of the Flag, which mandates, according to NASA spokesperson Elsie Diven Weigel, that

> "...when the aircraft achieves the desired altitude...the field of stars placement on each piece of aircraft in the U.S. must face the flow of the aircraft."

Submitted by Mark Ambrose of Park Ridge, Illinois.

$\mathcal{What}$ Is the Significance of the Indian and Star on Some Tootsie Roll Pop Wrappers? Why Are They on Only Some of the Wrappers?

We spoke to a public relations specialist at Tootsie Roll Industries, who reports that her department has been bombarded for decades with queries demanding to know the cosmic meaning of the little Indian boy depicted on the Tootsie Pop wrapper, shooting an arrow at a star. Some believe that you can win a prize if you find an Indian on your wrap; others think that the boy and star are symbols, usually benign ones.

But our source insists that there is nothing cosmic or metaphysical about this cartoon. For it rests alongside other depictions of children participating in activities like baseball, football, and bicycling. The wrappers' drawings have been unchanged for decades.

The cartoons reside on long bolts of paper, not unlike wallpaper. There are more different cartoons on the scroll than will appear on any one wrapper. The wrappers are cut from the scroll, not to highlight particular drawings but simply to cover the Pop. So the

Indian appears on only some Pops, just as the fishing or baseball pictures will be on some but not all wrappers.

Perhaps to forestall endless nagging questions, Tootsie Roll Industries sends out "Legend of the Indian Wrapper" to consumers who ask about this question, written by "Chief Shooting Star." Here is the *Reader's Digest* version of the legend.

Long ago, a man who owned a candy store wanted to make a new kind of lollipop, with a chewy candy center inside. He had no luck until, one night, a flash of light appeared in his bedroom. He awoke to find an Indian chief smiling at him. The chief promised to give the man the secret to his lollipop dream if he vowed never to stop making the candy.

The chief walked to the window, where there was one twinkling star in the sky. The chief pulled out a magical bow and arrow and launched the arrow at the star. As the man watched the flight of the arrow, another flash of light covered the chief. The man closed his eyes when confronted by the brilliant light, but when he reopened them, the chief had vanished. When he went to the window, the solitary star was replaced by a full moon.

The next day, the man returned to his shop and saw that his round lollipops now had chewy centers. The chief had come through, so the man kept his promise and continued to sell his special lollipops with the chewy center:

> "But the legend has it that once in a while the grand chief goes to the man's shop to check and see if the man has continued to keep his promise. The 'Indian Wrapper' is supposedly a sign that the grand chief has personally checked that particular lollipop for the chewy candy center."

Not a plausible explanation, perhaps, but no less true than the speculation that has always swirled around the mysterious Indian brave.

Submitted by Gina Del Giorgio of Chico, California. Thanks also to Steven Steuck of Minneapolis, Minnesota.

Why Is "Par Avion" Used to Designate "Air Mail" Even in English-Speaking Countries? Is French the International Language of Mail?

↬ We knew it was the language of love, but little did we know that French was the parlance of post offices. Michael F. Spates, manager of delivery for the United States Postal System, explains why:

> "Virtually every country in the world is a member of the Universal Postal Union (UPU), which governs and sets the terms for mailing between countries. The language of the UPU is French and the term 'Par Avion,' which dates back to before World War II, is the chosen designation for air mail."

The United States is a member of UPU, which is based not in France, but in Bern, Switzerland.

Submitted by Regina Earl of Pendleton, South Carolina.

SHOES. We can't live without them, but why do we have to be so obsessed with them? We get more questions about shoes than any other article of clothing, so we thought we'd try to give several Imponderables about shoes the boot.

Why Aren't Shoes Laced Up When You Try Them On in Stores?

❧ We learned how to tie our shoes when we were four. But no one ever taught us how to lace up a shoe from scratch. And continuing education programs don't seem to offer classes on the subject. Our assumption was that this shoe store practice was simply to annoy and humiliate us, but indeed, the experts we consulted named four reasons for leaving shoelaces unlaced:

1. Lacing shoes is labor-intensive and can't be done by machine. Therefore, it would be an added expense.

2. Different customers have special preferences in lacing techniques. Shoe consultant and historian William A. Rossi told us that "shoes are left unlaced to allow the buyer to choose his or her own lacing 'style.' "

3. It allows customers to try on shoes with easy entry. Some buyers interpret any difficulty in putting on a shoe as indicating that the shoe is too small.

4. Perhaps the most important consideration is psychological. Florsheim's N. B. Albert indicates that, subliminally, the unlaced shoe is "brand new." Stan Sterenberg, owner of an Athlete's Foot store in New York City, reports that a few customers refuse to buy any shoes that are already laced. After all, who knows who's been trying on the shoes before you?

Submitted by Karen E. Riddick of Dresden, Tennessee.

Why Have the Laces on Running/Athletic Shoes Gotten So Long? Are You Supposed to Tie Them Differently From "Regular" Shoelaces?

❧ Thank you, readers, for bringing up another issue that induces anxiety in us lace-impaired folks. After graciously allowing shoe salespersons to lace our shoes for us, it seems as if we are still left with enough excess material to rope a few steers.

We remember the good old days when athletic shoes had a nice straight line of holes along the edge of the instep. Now there are so many holes and eyelets on the high-tech athletic footwear, and in such random order, that the shoes look like connect-the-dot puzzles.

So what gives? Some of the impetus for longer-length laces was inspired by fads. For a while, long, untied laces were *de rigueur* among the hip-hop set. Before that, around-the-ankle lacing was popular among runners.

But the main reason why laces on athletic shoes will be around for the foreseeable future is the insidious philosophy of "variable lacing." Nike introduced "variable-width lacing" many years ago, as its public relations representative, Dusty Kidd, explains:

> "Shoes are subjected to considerable lateral and rotational forces on a basketball court, on the tennis court or on a trail run. To provide the best protection against injury, it is important that they have maximum stability. With two series of eyelets, one on a narrow pattern and the other on a wide pattern, variable-width lacing allows several lacing options, and that in turn provides a better fit."

If you complain about what we "vanilla lacers" are supposed to do with excess length, experts will start enumerating the many different ways to rid oneself of the excess, including putting the lace through the last eyelet twice.

Yep, that takes care of much of the excess length. Of course, it also eliminates any chance of removing or putting on the shoe without contracting a hernia, but . . .

Submitted by Peter J. Murphy of Yonkers, New York. Thanks also to Sam Bardo of Bristol, Indiana; Mick Donna of Fairfield, Ohio; Susan Engelmann of Fairway, Kansas; and Ken Fortuna of Wyandotte, Michigan.

What Is the Origin of Penny Loafers? And What Possessed Girls to Stick Coins in Their Shoes?

❧ The penny loafer is modeled after a Norwegian peasant fishing shoe (that's where the name "Weejuns" comes from) that had no numismatic interest whatsoever. According to clothing historian and consultant G. Bruce Boyer, the shoes became popular with young people in the United States in the mid-1930s, and enjoyed a special panache because they were originally brought back from Europe.

None of the experts could pinpoint the first genius to place a penny in the slit of the inset strap, but most speculated that it started on campus. N. B. Albert, an executive at Florsheim Shoe Company, was closest to having a conviction. He told us that originally the preferred coins were dimes rather than pennies, and were planted on the shoe by college girls to assure

> "that they always had carfare. Pennies were later used as decoration. The original design did not anticipate coins."

And why this need to put the pennies into the strap to begin with? Perhaps this is in the realm of metaphysics or psychology rather than history. Jack Herschlag, of the National Association of Men's Sportswear Buyers, was around during the penny loafer craze of the 1940s, and offers this universal theory:

> "Kids, like nature, abhor a vacuum. Was there ever an infant who could resist putting a hairpin into an electric outlet? Probably one kid did it and the others copied. Kids like to copy, too."

Submitted by Rebecca Schader of Westfield, New Jersey. Thanks also to Jim Yoakum of Atlanta, Georgia; and Anne Spence Core of Chevy Chase, Maryland.

Do the Holes on Wing-tip Shoes Serve Any Practical Function?

They certainly do. They make the shoes look pretty.

Shoe manufacturers refer to the holes as perforations or "perfs." N. B. Albert, of Florsheim Shoe Company, says the perforations were originally designed as a decoration to accentuate the shape of the wing tip.

And although once associated primarily with the toes of wing tips, perfs have spread to women's and even children's shoes, and have migrated to other parts of footwear, according to shoe industry consultant and historian Dr. William A. Rossi:

> "Wing tips are used not only on the toe but sometimes at the back of the shoe, or around the top rim, etc."

Submitted by Randall Buie of Henderson, Nevada.

David Feldman

TO
WHITE
HOUSE

TREASURY
SECRETARY

THE ACTUAL
TREASURER

TO
U.S.
MINT

Down the hall somewhere in Washington...

Why Is the Treasurer of the United States Always a Woman?

✦ Who is better qualified to answer this Imponderable than the current Treasurer of the United States, Mary Ellen Withrow? She was kind enough to write to us about how the tradition began:

> "The honorable Georgia Neese Clark of Richland, Kansas, was appointed to be the first woman to be Treasurer of the United States on June 4, 1949, by former President Harry Truman. Former Secretary of the Treasury John W. Snyder called her appointment 'a proper recognition of the prominent role women are playing in the public life of our nation.' "

We haven't been able to find what motivated Truman, nor why future presidents kept up the tradition, but they have been consistent: The next fifteen treasurers since Clark have all been women.

Becky Lowenthal, of the Treasury's public relations department, told *Imponderables* that critics have contended that the placement of women at the helm of the Treasury has smacked of tokenism, a way of forestalling carping about the lack of progress of women in other government positions. Lowenthal counters that regardless of the motivation, having a woman lead the Treasury has facilitated the progress of other women in the department, more so than other governmental offices.

Lowenthal mentioned that Ms. Withrow was heavily involved in marketing and in overseeing the manufacturing process, both of which are stereotypically male-oriented tasks, particularly since the world of money and finance has traditionally been dominated by men. Yet, at any time, the one female stronghold of upper-echelon government service could be yanked away, as Treasurer Withrow concedes:

> "The appointment of Georgia Neese Clark was the beginning of a tradition that has lasted forty-two years. Keep in mind, this tradition is not written in stone and is subject to change in the future."

Submitted by Michael Krawczak, United States Navy.

Why Are Canned Peaches Often Packed in Pear Juice?

⌬ Back in the paleolithic age, canned peaches were sweetened in heavy syrup. Then, in deference to consumer preferences for a less sweet and cloying taste (and fewer calories), light syrup was introduced. But health-conscious customers soon demanded "all-natural" sweeteners, and marketers understood the appeal of being able to trumpet "no sugar added" on labels.

With some fruits, such as pineapple, the natural juice is abundant and an excellent "packaging agent." But the problems with peach juice are numerous. A peach simply doesn't yield much juice, according to Tom Elliott of the Canned Fruit Promotion Service. As a result, peach juice concentrate is both expensive and not readily available, according to a spokesperson for the California

Cling Peach Advisory Board. Furthermore, although peach juice is naturally sweet, it doesn't have much peach flavor.

To the rescue comes pear juice. It is extremely sweet and readily available, and best of all, has a neutral flavor. Elliott mentions that you can use pear juice to pack such disparate fruits as apples, peaches and plums, without worrying about the liquid adding its own strong flavor.

Grape juice is even more plentiful than pear juice as a sweetening agent, and it is used to sweeten everything from granola bars to junk food. Roger Coleman, of the National Food Processors Association, says that some marketers are using apple and pineapple juices as well, sometimes blending them, depending upon availability and cost. But Coleman reports that more and more canned peach companies have overcome the technical and economic problems of packing fruits in their own juice. So it is sometimes possible to find canned peaches packed in, of all things, peach juice.

Submitted by Leanne Kisilevich of Edmonton, Alberta.

Who Was Absorbine Sr.? Why Is the Liniment Called "Absorbine Jr."?

❧ There *was* an Absorbine Sr. Sort of. Actually there still *is* an Absorbine Sr. Sort of.

The saga of Absorbines Junior and "Senior" all lead back to the end of the nineteenth century and our hero, Wilbur Young, a piano salesman who had an interest in horses. A century ago, horses were routinely used as basic transportation and to haul heavy farm equipment. Noting that horses have sensitive skin and muscles, Young concocted a liniment in his bathtub to relieve their assorted aches and pains.

Young's friends were delighted with the effect of the liniment upon their horses, and soon the demand for Wilbur's invention exceeded his bathtub's supply. Young turned the operation into a serious business and dubbed his liniment Absorbine. It wouldn't have made much sense to call his horse liniment Absorbine Sr., for Absorbine was the first product of what became W. F. Young, Inc.

Much to Young's surprise, people started rubbing Absorbine on their *own* bodies to relieve aches. Young was no fool. In the early 1900s, he launched Absorbine Jr., targeted for humans. And Jr. eventually outstripped its "father's" sales (we would guess that consumers tend to care about their own pains more than those of their equine buddies).

Absorbine still exists today for the veterinary market. Meanwhile, W. F. Young provides some line extensions for its Jr. brand ("regular," "extra-strength," and "antifungal"). One other piece of W. F. Young trivia is of cultural import: In order to prove the product's antifungal medication was effective, the company coined the term "athlete's foot" in 1940.

Submitted by Cheryl Lewis of Kingston, Ontario.

David Feldman

Why Is There a Lull or Stillness in the Air Just Before Tornadoes Strike?

We've heard many tornado survivors assert that the cliché "the lull before the storm" was true in their experience, and that mass destruction was preceded by an eerie stillness. We sought the counsel of Todd Glickman, assistant executive director of the American Meteorological Society and meteorologist for WCBS-AM in New York City, for the solution to this quandary:

> "Tornadoes need warm, moist air near the ground; cool, dry air aloft, and a force to 'kick' them off—that can often be a strong wind blowing many miles up in the atmosphere. But tornadoes are extremely local events. They affect relatively small areas at a time, and are characterized by strong upward and downward winds. And while tornadoes can move along at speeds ranging from a few to forty or fifty miles per hour, governed mainly by the speed of the parent thunderstorm across

the ground, the outward-blowing winds can dissipate fairly rapidly as one moves away from the thunderstorm."

Kenneth Kunkel, of the Midwestern Climate Center, notes that wind speed decreases before strong thunderstorms strike, whether or not they produce tornadoes:

> "Field observations and computer model simulations show that these relative lulls in winds at the ground occur near the front edge of the updraft of the thunderstorm. The winds at the surface turn upward as they are drawn into the thunderstorm so that there is less horizontal wind.
>
> "Warm air from the south meets cold air moving in from the northwest. The collision of these two air masses forces air upward to form thunderstorms. At the point of collision, warm air at the surface moving north is slowed by the oncoming cold front and is forced upward into the thunderstorm. This situation is quite temporary, since the cold front pushes the thunderstorm and the point of collision where the lull occurs rapidly eastward. The wind speed at the surface may not actually go to zero. However, it will appear to be very small in contrast to the strong winds occurring after the cold front passes."

Glickman assures *Imponderables* readers, though, that the lull is not universal:

> "Strong, gusty winds can, and often do, precede tornadoes."

Submitted by a caller on Ross Reynolds's KUOW-FM radio show in Seattle, Washington.

David Feldman

$\mathcal{W}hy$ Do Kool-Aid Packages Warn You Not to Keep Kool-Aid Stored in Metal Containers?

✎ Don't worry. You won't keel over if you drink Kool-Aid stored in a metal container. And don't be cynical. The instructions are not motivated by a kickback from Rubbermaid.

The instructions are just a gentle reminder that Kool-Aid has a tendency to absorb metallic taste from the container. You'll be much more likely to enjoy the pristine taste of Kool-Aid if you keep it in a more neutral vessel.

But if the thought of storing Kool-Aid in a glass or plastic container horrifies you, a consumer information specialist at Kraft had a piece of advice: "Try stainless steel." It's the one metal whose "taste" won't migrate to the drink.

Submitted by Julie Peterson of Raleigh, North Carolina.

$\mathcal{W}hy$ Do Newspapers Yellow So Much Faster Than Other Kinds of Paper?

✎ As the old *Lou Grant* opening credits aptly illustrated, about all old newspapers are good for is lining birdcages, which, we guess, was a 1970s notion of recycling. As West Virginia University journalism professor Theodore Lustig put it,

> "The newspaper publishers' principal concern is to get the news to their readers as fast as possible, but at the cheapest cost to them. That is why they use the cheapest papers and the cheapest inks. Almost every other type of paper is better made."

Newsprint falls into the category of "groundwood" paper, the lowest rung of the paper ladder, as Marcia A. Watt, preservation librarian at the Yale University Library, explains:

> "The primary components of wood are cellulose and lignin. Cellulose is long fibered and strong. It remains strong in a neutral or slightly alkaline environment. Cellulose is the primary component of cotton and flax. This is why papers composed entirely of these plants remain supple and white over time.
>
> "Lignin [better known as "sap"] is what makes wood hard, but it is also an acid. Newspaper is composed almost entirely of groundwood, wood that has not been chemically cooked, merely ground up.
>
> "The cooking process removes lignin and it is the lignin content of groundwood that quickly yellows on exposure to light. In addition, the acidic lignin breaks down the molecular structure of cellulose, thus weakening the paper."

Yellowing is no longer confined just to newspapers, though. Merrill Brown, of Crane Business Papers, reports that books increasingly have a yellowing problem too. More books of late have been printed on wood-pulp papers, whereas most books prior to World War II utilized cotton-linen fibers, which do not have lignin in them. Of course, books utilize superior inks and are printed on wood pulp that is treated chemically to avoid yellowing.

Ecological concerns about the toxicity of inks in newspapers might lead to the alleviation of the yellowing problem. According to Lustig, the pressure is on for newspapers to switch to solventless inks that do not pollute the atmosphere during printing. Not only are these inks more expensive, they require a higher grade of paper. Although new technology has made color printing affordable for many newspapers, no publisher wants all that money thrown into expensive ink to be set against paper tinged with that ugly shade of yellow.

Submitted by Bonnie Catto of South Hadley, Massachusetts. Thanks also to Tommy Campisi of Palos Verdes Estates, California.

David Feldman

$W\!hy$ Do Gorillas Pound Their Chests?

❧ Gorillas in the wild pound their chests for one fundamental reason: It scares the bejeezus out of other gorillas as much as it scares us.

The definitive study of chest-beating in gorillas was reported in G. B. Schaller's *Mountain Gorilla: Ecology and Behavior.* Schaller identifies a nine-step ritual of aggression in a fixed order: hooting; symbolic feeding; rising (the gorilla stands on two feet); throwing (usually throwing vegetation up in the air); chest-beating (usually two to twenty beatings, with open hands—sometimes accompanied by pounding of stomach or thighs, as well); leg kick (often, gorillas kick one leg in the air while chest-beating); running (usually sideways, first on two legs, then on all fours); slapping and tearing vegetation; and ground-thumping (a single thump with one or both palms usually culminates the ritual).

Only silverback males will exhibit all nine behaviors, but virtually any chest-beating will be accompanied by at least one of these other behaviors. Female gorillas have been observed chest-thumping in the wild, too.

So when and why do they do it? Gorillas are most likely to pound their chests in the following situations:

1. According to Susan Lumpkin, director of communications of the Friends of the National Zoo, chest-beating occurs most often when

> "a silverback (adult) male leading a group of females meets a potential rival for the affections of his females. Usually the rival is a lone silverback or, less often, another silverback with a female group."

2. Dominant gorillas use chest-beating in order to establish dominance and status within a troop.
3. Chest-beating is a not too subtle way for gorillas to mark territory when challenged by another troop.
4. Location signal. In his book *Gorillas*, Colin Groves mentions that when one male chest-beats, he is likely to be answered. So one of the functions of chest-beating might be as simple as a way of keeping the group together to avoid contact with other, less friendly, bands of animals. Gorillas usually avoid physical confrontations, so the bombast of chest-beating masks their peaceful inclinations.
5. Gorillas often perform the ritual when approached by people.
6. Excitement. In her book *Gorillas in the Mist*, Dian Fossey reports that chest-beating can simply be a signal for excitement or alarm.

Schaller also observed that gorillas will mimic the chest-beating displays of others and sometimes do it as play.

Evidently, gorillas can sort out when chest-beating is meant as a threat and when it is done for play. Indeed, at zoos we have observed a phenomenon described by Ed Hansen, president of the American Association of Zoo Keepers:

"[Chest-beating] is a learned behavior, so you will often see young animals clumsily displaying this behavior in an attempt to imitate their elders."

Actually, there is disagreement among experts about whether chest-beating is learned behavior simply because gorillas raised in captivity exhibit chest-beating. Groves claims that the behavior is innate and not copied, arguing that lone gorillas raised in captivity chest-beat.

Perhaps the most interesting response we received was from Francine Patterson, president and research director of the Gorilla Foundation. The foundation has received enormous attention for its Project Koko, what it calls "the longest continuous interspecies communication project of its kind in the world." Project Koko, launched in 1972, has been a long-range attempt to teach Koko American Sign Language. Although two other gorillas are involved, Koko has shown the most intellectual capability—she has a working vocabulary of more than 500 signs and has emitted more than 400 more. Koko understands approximately 2,000 words and has a tested IQ of between 70 and 95 on human scales.

Yet even the "intellectual" Koko and her two fellow gorilla-scholars still chest-beat when playing both with each other and with their human caregivers. Dr. Patterson sent us a transcript of a charming exchange between Koko and her close friend, the late Barbara Chiller, one of the founders of the Gorilla Foundation:

> BARBARA: Okay, can you tell me how gorillas talk?
> (KOKO beats her chest)
> BARBARA: What do gorillas say when they are happy?
> KOKO: Gorilla hug. [expressed in sign language]
> BARBARA: What do gorillas say to their babies?
> (KOKO beats her chest).

Submitted by Jordan Dagen of La Grange, Illinois.

Why Are There Three Dimples on Automobile Headlamps?

✥ They may be cute, but they're not dimples. Actually they are studs called "aiming pads," and they're not for decoration. According to Richard Van Iderstine, group leader of the visibility and control division of the National Traffic Safety Administration,

> "These devices are used to attach an adapter and mechanical aimer to the headlamp to measure and adjust headlamp vertical and horizontal aim."

They are utilized as early as the installation on the assembly line, when auto manufacturers conduct tests not only to check the aim of the lights, but also photometric tests, which measure the illuminating power of the headlamps.

Vann H. Wilber, of the American Automobile Manufacturers Association, indicates that auto mechanics use the aiming pads as mounting points for

> "mechanical headlamp aiming tools. These studs form a mechanical aiming plane which aligns a special tool, thereby allowing a mechanic to check and, if necessary, re-aim the headlamp beam patterns."

Increasingly, new methods of mechanical aim are being utilized, so "dimples" are starting to disappear from many new cars.

Submitted by Hal Shoenfield of Brooklyn, New York. Thanks also to Bruce Rogers of Vestal, New York.

Why Do Many Linens Have an Unpleasant Smell When New?

❧ After receiving this Imponderable from Joe Schwartz, we had our own run-in with foul-smelling sheets. We must confess we've never mastered the fine art of folding sheets. (Is this what they taught girls in home economics classes while boys learned how to make metal notepaper-holders? We're confident that learning to make metal notepaper holders is a skill that would come in handy if we were to ever go into the profession of handcrafting notepaper holders, but linen-folding is a skill we need to master for our everyday lives.)

So when the rare houseguest ventures into *Imponderables* Central for an overnight stay, we often find it easier to buy a new set of sheets than to expose the guest's delicate sensibility to our linen closet, which resembles what the Blob would look like in a closet if it were made out of linen instead of industrial sludge.

But we digressed, didn't we? So the last time we had a guest over for the night, we whipped out some new, all-cotton sheets, and they smelled like a cross between a men's locker room and a manure processor's waste products in high season. We were forced to resort to the blob closet to equip the sofa bed.

Why inflict this olfactory nightmare upon an innocent public? According to B. A. Thorp, vice president of process technology at James River Corporation, the smell comes from starch or other sizing materials:

> "This product is less expensive than popular spray starches and can have an unpleasant odor and can cause some skin discomfort. . . ."

So why add the starch? Starch keeps the sheets wrinkle-free for display purposes. Although the sizing is used in the finishing of the linens, and helps provide a more pleasant feel and sheen, if it weren't for the need to seduce shoppers in the store, the sheets could be washed by the processor.

At least all these finishing materials are water soluble. Connie Parker, of the National Association of Institutional Linen Management, reports that one trip to the washing machine will dissolve and eliminate all the offending constituents. And in the process, of course, rendering them sweet-smelling and impossible to fold, at least if you are foldingly-impaired like us.

Submitted by Joe Schwartz of Troy, New York.

Why Do Some Keys Enter a Lock With the Teeth Up and Others With the Teeth Down? Why Isn't the Orientation Standardized?

❧ The orientation could be standardized. Actually, it is standardized. Usually. Allen Tyson, of Diebold Inc., explains:

> "The individual lock manufacturers through the years have made locks to their own design and there was never an organization or documentation to restrict how the keys fit into locks. Every manufacturer has its own way of engineering locks. Some locks are pin locks and some are wafer. Some locks are double cut, some have slotted keyways, and some are flat."

James Watt, the Northwest vice president of Associated Locksmiths of America, told us that in the United States, most pin tumbler lock designs require the lock cylinder to be oriented so that the teeth (or "bitings," as locksmiths call them) and key blade enter the pin tumbler cylinder facing up. However, most European lock cases incorporate a different design, so the bitings usually enter face down. Master locksmith Jerome Andrews commented wryly that even the Big Three carmakers can't get their acts straight: GM makes you insert the keys with bitings down; Chrysler has you put them in face up; and Ford (and many foreign makes) provides double-sided keys for those of us confused by the other two.

Some of our sources argue that the "bitings up" position is inherently superior, both because it tends to put less wear and tear on the tumbler, and because it leaves less dirt in the lock. Yet others point out that locks are "handed," and are sometimes turned "upside down" (with the bitings down) so that they can be installed in doors where the hinges are on the "wrong" side. As long as the key blade and bitings are oriented in the correct position for the pin tumbler cylinder, an "upside-down" lock will work properly.

So when we plumb the dirty depths of this Imponderable, we cannot help but believe that Watt's conclusion makes the most sense:

> "The main reason that not all pin tumbler lock cylinders in the U.S. are mounted with . . . the bitings in the up position is due to improper mounting in noncompliance with directed manufacturers' recommendations. Most locks in this country are installed, not by qualified professional locksmiths, but by contractors, handymen, supers, or do-it-yourselfers. Little time is given to the instructions, and therefore installations are not always correct."

Indeed, we couldn't help but be charmed by the admission of Richard Hudnut, product standards coordinator for the Builders Hardware Manufacturers Association, who evidently follows manufacturer specs the way we follow VCR setup manuals: "Most of us are not good at reading instructions and usually throw them away before the installation starts."

Submitted by Daniel Springer of Allentown, Pennsylvania.

Why Does Pepper Make Us Sneeze?

❧ Other hot, spicy foods make us wince, make us cringe, and make us cram huge quantities of cold liquids down our gullets. But why does only pepper make us sneeze?

The essential oils found in pepper are the culprit, according to Polly Murphy, manager of consumer affairs for McCormick and Company. These oils, which can be extracted from the berries of the pepper plant, are used by food processors to flavor sausages, sauces, salad dressings, processed meats, and many other foods.

But eating a sausage seasoned with pepper doesn't make you sneeze. The major culprit is piperine, a chemical found in black and white pepper. Thomas F. Burns, executive vice president of the American Spice Trade Association, explains:

> "Piperine provides the pleasant biting sensation that accompanies the aroma to the mouth when it is tasted. Since piperine bites the tongue, it obviously also bites the delicate membranes of the nose."

Other chilies also contain chemicals that "bite" much like piperine. Our table pepper, though, tends to be ground finely. When particles of, say, black pepper, are drawn into the nose, our body has the good sense to try to expel the particles, just as it would try to expel any other dust particles.

That's why Burns suggests, in the spirit of the James Bond entreaty that martinis should be "shaken, not stirred":

> "Pepper should be smelled, not sniffed. Its delicate aroma is one of its great attributes and can only be appreciated when inhaled slowly."

Submitted by Jason Glass of El Monte, California. Thanks also to A. Grossman of Cornwell Heights, Pennsylvania; Don Droppo of St. Paul, Minnesota; and Julie Peterson of Raleigh, North Carolina.

What Percentage of a Ripped Stamp Has to Be Intact to Be Considered Valid by the United States Postal System?

❧ Believe it or not, there is no set percentage. But don't try affixing itsy-bitsy stamp fragments to an envelope. It won't fool the machines used by the USPS, as Michael F. Spates, manager of delivery, explains:

> "Postage stamps use a number of phosphorus strips, which are invisible to the naked eye, to trigger canceling equipment. For the most part, a stamp must be intact in order to trigger the mechanisms. If a piece of mail is rejected at the canceling stage of processing, it will most likely be returned to sender for correct postage."

We also posed this Imponderable to Jeffrey H. Zelkowitz, senior counsel for classification and customer service at the USPS. He noted that the Domestic Mail Manual allows a postal employee to refuse stamps that are "mutilated or defaced." But another DMM provision allows a consumer to exchange a damaged stamp for a valid, intact stamp.

So the bottom line, as Zelkowitz concedes, is "revenue protection." The USPS isn't sanguine about folks attempting to rip up one stamp and exchange the pieces for two stamps or affix them to two different envelopes.

We have to admit that we can't disagree with Zelkowitz's assessment of the USPS's policy: "I would normally expect this provision to be administered in a commonsense manner." "USPS" and "commonsense" in the same sentence with no sarcasm intended. What a concept.

Submitted by Gerald Rosenbaum of New York, New York.

Why Don't the Palms of Our Hands or the Soles of Our Feet Get Sunburned?

❦ It doesn't take a brain surgeon, or a dermatologist, for that matter, to understand that in order to get a part of the body sunburned, it has to come in contact with the sun. Think about how your palms and soles are positioned in your everyday life, and you'll realize the difficulty in burning our palms or soles.

When you are walking outdoors, the palms are exposed not to the sun, but pressed against your clothing. The soles are covered with socks and shoes.

Even if you go to Sunburn City, the beach, the palms and soles are likely to get less exposure to the sun than other parts of the body. The palms are usually pressed against the sand when lying down (in our observation, virtually everyone keeps their palms down when lying on their back, and most do when lying on their stomach, too, possibly because symbolically the palms-up position suggests defenselessness). The soles, even if exposed, are usually kept at an angle to the sun, much less vulnerable than the torso or the face. All things being equal, there aren't any parts of the unclothed body less likely to burn than the soles or palms.

But all things are not equal, as Worcester, Massachusetts, dermatologist Gerald C. Gladstone explains:

"The skin on the palms and soles is much thicker than elsewhere on the body. Approximately 50 percent of the skin's ability to filter out and protect itself from burning ultraviolet rays is in the outermost tiny fraction of a millimeter of skin, the *stratum corneum* (the compact outermost portion of the epidermis), which is composed of so-called 'dead' skin cells packed together in a tight layer.

"Because this particular layer is especially thick on the palms and the soles, and in fact is thicker on the heel portion of the sole than anywhere else on the body, its filtering effect for ultraviolet rays is much greater in these locations, so that sunburn rarely develops there."

Still, burning *is* possible in the soles and palms. Many skin doctors use ultraviolet A radiation to treat certain diseases, and Samuel T. Selden, a dermatologist practicing in Chesapeake, Virginia, reports that

> "this longer wavelength of sunlight can penetrate easily through the thickened skin on palms and soles and burn them quite readily. But most individuals go through their lives without experiencing sunburn on their palms and soles because of the anatomical difficulty of aiming these surfaces toward the sun."

Lexington, Kentucky, dermatologist Joe Bark adds that even if held in direct sunlight long enough to burn,

> "the undersides of the wrists would burn painfully long before the palms, thereby inducing someone to escape the sun long before the palmar burning would normally occur."

We did find at least one live human being who has endured the indignity of suffering from sole-burn. Beth Laiderman, an ex-lifeguard in Minneapolis, sat at her station every day during the summer, with her bare feet straight in front of her, exposed to the sun. Although her palms and soles didn't get quite as dark as the rest of her body, she put it this way: "If the rest of my body was well done, my soles were medium-well."

Submitted by Diane Watterson of New Orleans, Louisiana.

DON'T GET SO WOUND UP!

OH, YEAH! LOOK WHO'S CROSS!!

Buns 75¢ | Rolls 60¢

Disgruntled Breakfast Pastry

What's the Difference Between a Bun and a Roll?

❧ The U.S. Food and Drug Administration stipulates only that breads weigh more than one-half pound per unit and that rolls and buns weigh less than one-half pound. All three starches must be yeast-leavened bakery product. But the FDA draws no distinction between buns and rolls.

And neither do retail bakeries. One company's "hamburger buns" is another's "hamburger rolls."

But a few sketchy observations can be made. Tom Lehmann, our trusty source at the American Institute of Baking, while conceding that there is no clear-cut answer to this Imponderable, passed along a short write-up that the Institute prepared:

> "The term 'roll' is generally applied to filled products, especially those that are formed by sheeting and rolling-up or folding the dough, such as cinnamon rolls [which, in many areas, are sold as cinnamon buns] and Danish rolls. There are exceptions to this, however, in that hard-crusted products are

also included in the roll category. Products of this type include Kaiser rolls and French rolls.

"Buns, on the other hand, are generally more bread-like in shape (round or elongated) and typically do not contain a filling. The one notable exception to this is the Easter favorite, hot-cross buns."

Simon Jackel, director of Plymouth Technical Services, concurs with the Institute, but argues that it might be more accurate to contrast them by indicating that buns are usually soft, and that rolls can be hard or soft. But ultimately, Jackel muses that pinpointing the answer to this question is "sort of like asking: 'Is it a hamburger or a chopped-beef patty?' "

Submitted by Robert Lawler of Ivyland, Pennsylvania.

Why Are the Ceilings of Train Stations So High?

When we think of high-ceilinged train stations, we tend to conjure up landmarks such as Grand Central Terminal in New York or Union Station in Washington, D.C. But the poser of this Imponderable lives in Rhinebeck, New York. Rhinebeck is a stop on Amtrak's schedule. We've been there. Rhinebeck has a small station —with a high ceiling.

How did this strange tradition begin? John Horvath, of the United Transportation Union, lent not only his own expertise but also that of railroad buffs and professionals on the Internet Usenet and CompuServe TrainNet Forum. A consensus formed about two points of historical import.

The first and most popular theory was that stations have high ceilings for purely practical reasons. Many train stations were built in the days of steam locomotives. As Horvath puts it,

"The high ceilings gave the smoke and steam, that would otherwise choke boarding and departing passengers, somewhere to go and helped ventilate the building."

The second theory hearkens back to an era that seems not only bygone but prehistoric. Horvath reports:

"Two respondents drew parallels between older rail stations and the cathedrals of Europe. Each noted that the buildings were a testament to the dominant 'faiths' of the times in which they were built. Rail stations were the public face of mankind's progress, reflecting the prevailing faith in industry and serving as 'temples' celebrating the fruits of the Industrial Revolution. Railroading at the time represented one of the most ambitious organizational undertakings in history, one that touched on and transformed all aspects of society.

". . . Stations were built in a grandiose manner because the times and the economies could afford grandiose expression. In other words, labor and materials were cheaper, so they built stations in a grandiose manner because they *could*."

Denis J. Bergquist, a railroad safety consultant, concurs that the magnificent stations were indeed built as monuments to the wealth and power of the railroads, but adds that there is an important logistical advantage of a high-ceilinged station today: Not only does the high ceiling provide passengers and employees relief from the congestion of a busy station, but it enables the railroad to post track numbers and departure times above the assembled throng.

Submitted by Frances Balcomb of Rhinebeck, New York.

SPECIAL THANKS to our cyberspace sources: Russell G. Bates; Max Wyss; Michael Sproule; Bob Ciminel; Robert Coe; Clem Tillier; Chris Vernell; Gerry Foley; Matthew Mitchell; Ernest H. Robl; Tim Smith; Jeremy Featherstone; Bill Bedford; Dave Pierson; Tobias Benjamin Koehler; and Rob Hoffer.

What Do Ticks in the Forest Live on When They Don't Have Humans to Eat?

❧ You needn't worry about ticks. Like a resourceful dieter, ticks seem to find *something* to eat.

Approximately 800 species of ticks have evolved that feed on vertebrates, according to Leslie Saul-Gershenz, insect zoo director of the San Francisco Zoological Society. Although a few species of ticks will bite humans, other delicacies for ticks include birds, bats, rabbits, lizards, deer (the tiny deer tick is responsible for spreading Lyme disease), dogs, horses, small rodents, and anything else that moves with blood coursing through its veins.

Although specific species of ticks have certain preferences for mammalian hosts, they are not exclusive. If a tick that normally feeds on horses has no equine possibilities, it might condescend to suck a human's blood.

And if they prefer, ticks can choose to be picky, for they need to feed less often than many other insects and arachnids. According to Karen Yoder, certification manager of the Entomological Society of America,

> "If no hosts are available, ticks can actually survive for several months without a blood meal. Brown dog ticks have been recorded surviving as long as 200 days without a blood meal."

No species of tick feeds exclusively (or even primarily) on humans, so don't justify your next trip to the forest as a rescue mission for these enterprising arachnids.

Submitted by Daniel Springer of Allentown, Pennsylvania.

Why Don't Male Ballet Dancers Dance "On Pointe"?

✤ Why do only ballerinas have the thrill of torturing their toes when dancing? This masochistic tradition dates back nearly two hundred years. According to Margot C. Lehman, past president of the American Dance Guild, the first known print of a dancer on pointe is from 1821.

But the groundbreaking moment came a decade later. Elsa Posey, president and director of Posey School of Dance, explains:

> "Pointe shoes and pointe technique and the art of dancing 'sur les pointes' began in the 1830s. The first full-length ballet danced en pointe was *La Sylphide* of 1832, starring Marie Taglioni, whose father is sometimes credited with inventing the stiffening of the ballet shoe to enable her to appear to be floating or flying with lightness and delicacy."

Soon, Taglioni and her pink satin slippers became the dance personification of womanhood. Rebecca Hutton, executive director of the National Dance Association, told *Imponderables* that choreographers prized on pointe dancing because it made ballerinas taller and yet more ethereal. Indeed, the toes of ballerinas became the weapon to launch what we now call the "Romantic Era," as Margot Lehman amplifies:

> "The Romantic ballet, a reflection of the Romantic Era's concern with the ethereal and the exotic, had as a main theme the escape from the real world into the world of the supernatural—a world of ghosts, spirits, and sprites unconstrained by gravity. Lightness and grace were seen and developed as the essential female qualities. Toe dancing became one of the most important tools of the Romantic ballet to help dancers create the illusion of weightlessness."

Giselle, A Midsummer Night's Dream, Coppelia, The Nutcracker, Firebird, Swan Lake, and *Sleeping Beauty* are but a few of the ballets with featured female roles danced on pointe.

There is absolutely no anatomical distinction between the sexes that would make females better able to dance on pointe. If you look hard enough, you can find men on their toes. Lehman suggests many anomalies:

> "The British choreographer Frederick Ashton choreographed for on-pointe male dancers in a feature film about the world of Beatrix Potter. His dancers were from the Royal Ballet and wore toe shoes in their roles as dancing mice and other delightful creatures. The all-male American Trocadero Ballet does tongue-in-cheek versions of *Swan Lake* and other ballet classics on pointe and in tutus. And the male dancers of the Republic of Georgia dance on the tips of their boots while performing athletic ethnic and folk material. . . ."

Posey adds that often the parts of the stepsisters in *Cinderella* and Bottom in *A Midsummer Night's Dream* are played by males on pointe.

All the experts we consulted indicated that it is not uncommon for men to participate in the "pointe" segment of class, whether to strengthen their feet, stretch their arches, to discover the change of balance entailed in order to become better partners for their ballerinas, or even, as Rebecca Hutton reports Baryshnikov does, just to have fun.

But these exceptions prove the rule. Dancing on pointe is associated not only with females but with femininity itself. While fewer contemporary than Romantic ballets require ballerinas to dance on pointe, there is also a trend among modern choreographers to emphasize male dancers' strength and athleticism. Daintiness is out.

The ethereality of dancing on pointe is achieved only through intense training and specialized equipment. The toe shoe, according to Lehman,

"is a satin slipper with a thin, stiff leather sole and a hardened box at the tip which encases the toes. The dancers often pad the inside of this toe box with lamb's wool for comfort and extra protection. The point of contact with the floor is this tip—about the size of a silver dollar—which must carry the body's entire weight."

The tip of the shoe is hardened by the gluing together of layers of material. The box of the shoe covers the dancers' toes tightly, so that, in effect, as Posey puts it,

"the body weight is transferred through the structure of the foot as a single unit."

If there is anything we learned from researching this Imponderable, it's "Don't try this at home." Elsa Posey, who has researched and written about dance education for the young, warns that the shoes alone can't provide sufficient protection for fledgling ballerinas:

"A contraction of the muscles of the feet, ankles, legs, and torso enables the dancers to 'push' themselves upwards without injury to their feet. No one should attempt to dance on pointe without years of practice."

Most juvenile ballerinas should not even attempt dancing on pointe until they are twelve or their feet have stopped growing. It's ironic that the very technique that conveys femininity and weightlessness requires brute strength. In this case, traditional sexual stereotypes have made life much easier for men.

Submitted by Sue Waldren of Papillion, Nebraska. Thanks also to Jeanne Salt of Tualatin, Oregon.

Why Does the U.S. Navy Use "BRAVO ZULU" or "BZ" to Indicate "Well Done"?

❦ The Allied Naval Signal Book, which lists and decodes the significance of signals, is theoretically a confidential publication, but some of its contents, such as the meaning of "BRAVO ZULU," have become commonly known. We received an informative letter from retired Navy captain George L. Graveson, Jr., now a public affairs director of the Naval Submarine League, that helped us understand the arcane language of the Navy:

> "Navy ships and aircraft communicate in various ways, from plain language by voice to encoded signals requiring machines to decipher the messages. The Navy uses many forms of communication, including: voice, radio, flashing light, semaphore, etc. Another method of conveying information is the *signal flag* between ships at sea.
> "Signal flags are used separately and in combination to pass information, to give and acknowledge orders and to identify situations or conditions which may be hazardous to other

vessels. There is a signal flag for each letter of the alphabet and others which signify certain frequently used terms or specify certain recurring events, such as maneuvering procedures.

"Some alphabet flags, in addition to their primary use, are also used to signal certain events. For instance, the BRAVO flag flown by itself indicates that the vessel on which it is flying is handling ammunition. The MIKE flag indicates that divers are working in the vicinity of the vessel, and so forth. Certain flags flown in combination with others constitute a sort of 'shorthand' way of making a statement or conveying information, based upon a dictionary of terms found in a signal book.

"[The signal book] is where BRAVO ZULU comes in. The flag hoist BRAVO ZULU or BZ means: Well Done. The use of the term has spilled over into oral and written communication throughout the Navy."

We still haven't figured out how using "BRAVO ZULU" on a radio saves anyone time or effort (indeed, there's one more syllable in "BRAVO ZULU" than in "Well Done"). But these "bigraphs" (combination signals) allow a greater vocabulary than could be conveyed by a mere twenty-six flags or initials.

This Imponderable obviously begs the question of how an irritated captain could communicate *dis*pleasure. The answer comes from retired Commander Alvin Grobmeier. The letter "N" or "Negat" is used to put a negative spin on any other signal. So NEGAT BRAVO ZULU means, "Not Well Done," although Grobmeier indicates that other colorful terms are used more frequently.

Submitted by M. B. Fraker of Tracy, California.

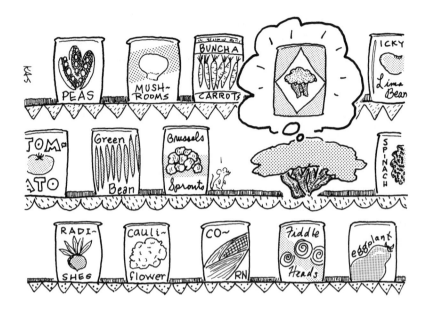

When Less Popular Vegetables Are Canned, Why Can't You Find Canned Broccoli?

Notwithstanding George Bush's aberrant preferences, the last two decades have shown enormous growth in the popularity of fresh broccoli. Medical experts sing its praises. So why can't you find broccoli in cans? Let us count the reasons why.

1. **Color.** In its natural state, broccoli florets have a vivid, dark-green color; the stalks are lighter and soothing in hue. But according to Joe Nucci of Mann Packing, when heated in hermetically sealed cans, the color comes out more like an ugly Army green, not unlike canned green peas—dull compared to their fresh counterparts. Even worse, the delicate leaves turn black when processed.

2. **Texture.** Most broccoli lovers prefer the vegetable *al dente;* to a

David Feldman

connoisseur, the broccoli should give your teeth and jaw a little fight. Roger Coleman, senior vice president of public communications for the National Food Processors Association, comments that "broccoli, like some other vegetables like cauliflower, does not hold up well in canning."

Remember those peas that canned broccoli resembled in color? Processed broccoli mimics canned peas' mushy texture when processed. Even peas have a skin to help preserve the integrity of texture, but broccoli, without any such protection, is vulnerable to heat.

We're sure that a brilliant reader is thinking: Why not cook the broccoli at low heat? After all, if we can steam a broccoli without turning it into a pile of desiccated green mush, why can't canners? The problem is that broccoli, like other members of the crucifer family (e.g., cauliflower, brussels sprouts, cabbage) is high in sulfur compounds. Dr. George York, of the University of California at Davis, told *Imponderables* that, once canned, all vegetables must be heated to 240–250 degrees in order to kill the spores that cause botulism. But this precaution causes unwanted side effects— the high heat also releases sulfur compounds. These sulfur compounds are responsible for rendering all crucifers virtually "uncannable."

York points out that pickled cauliflower is readily available. Pickling and the lower heat associated with placing vegetables into jars counteracts botulism and keeps the vegetables' structure intact while still retarding spoilage.

3. Availability of fresh and frozen broccoli. Dave Stidholf, of Mann Packing, indicates that unlike some of the more popular canned vegetables, fresh broccoli is readily available and relatively inexpensive all year long. Broccoli also freezes exceptionally well, so the vast majority of processed broccoli comes in frozen form.

4. Demand. Nucci told *Imponderables* that the market for canned vegetables overall is "remarkably flat," while fresh (and frozen) produce sales continue to boom. And there's a good reason for it. Not only does fresh produce taste better, it also retains vitamins and minerals lost in processing.

Even if your enthusiasm for broccoli resembles George Bush's, at least the "fresh poison" will make you healthier, if not any happier, than canned.

Submitted by Linda Phillips of Orlando, Florida.

Why Are the Athletes of DePaul University, a Catholic Institution, Known as the "Blue Demons"?

If Transylvania University decided to nickname its team the "Crimson Vampires," we could understand it. But why did an esteemed Catholic university choose the devil as its mascot?

We spoke to John Lanctot, sports information director of DePaul, who told *Imponderables* that the story of the school's mascot is downright benign. In fact, when the sports program began at DePaul, the board of directors didn't decide on a mascot at all.

DePaul was founded in 1898, and two years later first gave letters to players who had completed a year of varsity competition. What were athletes running around campus with huge "D"s on their sweaters called? In Chicago, "D-Men," evidently.

Over time, "D-Men" metamorphosed into "demon." The school later voted to color its mascot blue, to symbolize loyalty, completing the transformation of "D" lettermen into the current "Blue Demons."

Submitted by James Pastere of Lockport, Illinois.

Why Are University of North Carolina Players Called Tar Heels? And What in the Heck Is a Tar Heel?

Even if an incarnation of evil doesn't impress as the most positive of images, at least a Blue Demon sounds threatening and ominous. But are you likely to fear facing a Tar Heel, a competitor with dirty, sticky feet? Or dirty and sticky shoes?

We contacted the patient folks at the University of North Carolina at Chapel Hill, and found that we were far from the first to wonder about Tar Heels. But to our surprise, UNC historians aren't positive about the origins of the term either. Two legends predominate.

The first story revolves around British general Cornwallis's troops during the Revolutionary War. After fording a river in North Carolina, the British soldiers found their feet encased in tar. Crafty North Carolinians supposedly dumped tar to slow the progress of the British troops:

"The British were said to have observed that if you waded in North Carolina rivers you would get tar on your heels."

The second theory is that the nickname dates back to the Civil War. The legend states that some North Carolina boys chastised other Confederate troops for abandoning the battlefield in the heat of battle:

"The soldiers threatened to stick tar on the heels of the retreating soldiers to help them stay in the battle next time. General Lee is said to have commented, 'God bless the Tar Heel boys.' "

UNC's other most-often-asked question about their nickname can be answered more emphatically: "It is Tar Heel, not Tarheel."

Submitted by Larry Walker of Marietta, Georgia.

How Do Trees in Urban Areas That Are Covered With Concrete Get Enough Water to Grow?

☞ "Not very well," replies Drew Todd, urban forestry coordinator for the Ohio Department of Natural Resources. Indeed, nearly five percent of New York City's "street trees" die every year, far more than can be replaced, even though the city plants only the hardiest species. One of the main problems is that trees are usually an afterthought in most urban projects. In many cases, the tree is planted after the concrete has already been laid, so crews tear out a four-by-four-foot piece of concrete, put in a four-by-four-by-four planter, and hope for the best. Todd reports that the average life of a tree in urban environments is a sad four to seven years; trees planted in lawns tend to live much longer.

So many problems conspire to wreak havoc upon urban trees:

1. Insufficient soil and nutrients for growth.
2. Insufficient space for the root structure to grow. Something

has to give when roots expand below the surface of the ground—either the expanding roots will crack the sidewalk or their growth will be stunted.

3. Insufficient water or excess water. Trees require water to survive. But excess water can be almost as dangerous if water doesn't evaporate from the tree pit, "drowning" the tree and preventing it from using available oxygen.

4. Insufficient oxygen. This is a particular danger when a sidewalk is installed over the tree, "suffocating" the root structure. Lloyd Casey, rural forestry management specialist with the U.S. Forest Service, told *Imponderables* that the trees need enough air to capture a sufficient amount of carbon dioxide to eventually convert into oxygen.

5. Salt. In the East, salt used to treat roads is a particular menace to trees.

6. Heat. Concrete radiates heat, and the reflections from the glass in the city are also not good for the tree.

7. Pollution. Not just the smog and ozone hurt trees. So does what we will euphemistically call "doggy pollution."

8. Bumps and bruises. Pedestrians bump into trees and put stress on the trunk and root structure by tying heavy objects (such as bicycles) to them.

9. Changes in the tree's immediate environment. A simple road patch or sidewalk joint repair results in severing roots. Mature trees, with an established root structure, are particularly vulnerable to disruption, but according to Bill Kruidenier, of the International Society of Arboriculture, younger trees still have flexibility, and their roots will grow (usually *out* rather than *down)* to find the nutrients, oxygen, or water that they need.

Yet with all these obstacles, some trees somehow survive, even thrive, in the city, often as long as fifteen years or more. As Kruidenier puts it, "Trees are notorious for finding moisture." Roots of trees usually go down only about 30 to 36 inches, but will go lower if water is available. The city offers unique water sources close to the surface: the intentional heat-expansion cracks in the sidewalk; gutters; and natural cracks in man-made surfaces.

And trees are built to conserve water from the top of their ecosystem, too, as botanist Bruce Kershner explains:

> "Much of the rainwater that lands on branches gets directed down to the trunk, where it flows to the tree base and then into the roots. Thus the tree branch system acts as a funnel, concentrating the water."

Submitted by Ann Berger of Lake Ariel, Pennsylvania.

What's the Difference Between Low- and High-Altitude Tennis Balls?

Not much. Balls, like long jumper Bob Beamon in Mexico City, or baseballs off the bat of a Colorado Rockies slugger, travel higher and farther in high-altitude, low-air-pressure environments. Playing tennis in Aspen, Colorado, with a conventional tennis ball is a little like playing tennis with a Super Ball on steroids—exciting, but unpredictable.

To counter this problem, several of the major tennis-ball manufacturers market high-altitude tennis balls. In most cases, they use the same materials to build the balls—the same felt, the same inner core. The only difference is the internal pressure.

Jeff Miller, product manager of court sports for Spalding Sports Worldwide, told *Imponderables* that the typical "low-altitude" championship ball has an internal pressure between 12 and 14 psi. The high-altitude ball is rated at nearly half that, 6–8 psi (the air pressure in the can is also correspondingly lower on high-altitude balls).

Miller reports that most of the sales of high-altitude balls are in the state of Colorado, but a smattering of demand can be found in such far-flung areas as West Virginia and New Mexico.

Submitted by Dick Morton of Breckenridge, Colorado.

David Feldman

1. Before...   2. After!

Were Milk Duds Duds?

❧ When we're trying to select a title for our tomes, we are cognizant of the delicate sensitivities of our readers. For example, two of the candidates for the title of this book were "Do Swimmers Sweat?" and "Why Do Toads Have Warts?" Neither question conjures up the most pleasant image, and this was a major factor in choosing an alternative. Once we decided against them as titles, we weren't even inspired to research these gross-outs for this book.

It is with amazement, then, that we have always considered the name given to an enduring American candy classic, Milk Duds. If we had been given the assignment, we'd have called the product "Milk Neatos" or "Milk Perfectos." Why acknowledge in the name of your product that there is something amiss?

Luckily, Milton J. Holloway, who owned F. Hoffman & Company, which created Milk Duds in 1926, didn't have us around to consult, for the name of the candy does acknowledge that the end product wasn't quite what its creators had in mind. According to a representative at Leaf, Inc., who now owns the brand, the original idea was for Milk Duds to be perfectly round. But because of the consistency of the product, Holloway couldn't achieve his goal.

The nonuniform, homely, bite-sized pieces resisted any attempts to match the pristine spherical conception. Some anonymous visionary at the candy company thought of "dud" to describe the odd shape. And the "Milk" was added because from the start, the candy was loaded with milk.

Originally, the word "dud" was applied to a bomb or shell that didn't explode. Now it is ascribed to just about anything that is worthless. Milk Duds might be the only food product to attain success by trumpeting its imperfection on every package it sells.

Submitted by Heidi Zimmerman of San Diego, California.

Who Was the Henry That Inspired the Name of Oh Henry! Candy Bars?

A customer relations representative from Nestlé told *Imponderables* that many aficionados of Oh Henry!, the first nationally marketed candy bar, assume that the candy was named after author William Sydney Porter, who used the pseudonym O. Henry. Actually, the origin of the candy bar's name is as surprising as the endings for which Porter was noted.

Oh Henry! was first sold in 1920 by the Williamson Candy Company of Chicago. Williamson owned a retail-wholesale candy business, and employed quite a few young women; Nestlé attributes the unusual name of the confection to the attractiveness of these employees:

> "Every day a young fellow named Henry would come in and talk to the girls who worked there. The girls got into the habit of asking Henry to do odd jobs and favors for them, so you would always hear, 'Oh, Henry, would you get me this or that?'
>
> "When it was time to name the newly developed confec-

tion the salesmen commented that all they constantly heard around the store was 'Oh, Henry!' . . . so that's what they called it."

We can't swear that this story isn't apocryphal; it strikes us as exhibiting a keen imagination.

Submitted by Courtney Black of Bartlesville, Oklahoma.

Who Was Baby Ruth Named After?

❧ As long as we had Nestlé on the horn, we inquired about another of their products with a mysterious name. We were quickly disabused of the notion that the candy bar was named after Babe Ruth (who looked as if he consumed quite a few chocolate bars in his day). Baby Ruth was introduced shortly after Oh Henry! bars, in the early 1920s, by Curtiss Candy Company. And the origin of its name is far more concrete than Oh Henry!'s:

> "The name honors President and Mrs. Grover Cleveland's daughter, endearingly referred to as 'Baby Ruth.' The trademark was patterned exactly after the engraved lettering of the name used on a medallion struck for the Chicago World's Columbian Exposition in 1893 and picturing the President, his wife, and daughter Baby Ruth."

Why Did the Republicans Choose Andrew Johnson, a Democrat, to Be Abraham Lincoln's Running Mate in 1864?

❧ In 1860, Abraham Lincoln won the presidency along with running mate Hannibal Hamlin, a refugee from the Democratic Party. A member of the House of Representatives from Maine, Hamlin joined the Republicans in 1856 because of his strong antislavery convictions.

But in 1864, Lincoln changed horses. No president had gained reelection since Andrew Jackson in 1832. In 1864, Lincoln would have more formidable opposition than in 1860, when he beat John Breckinridge and a Democratic party divided over the slavery issue. In 1864, Democrats nominated popular General George B. McClellan, former commander-in-chief of the Union Army, as their presidential candidate. McClellan was relieved of his command when Lincoln became convinced that the general's lack of aggressiveness cost the Union victories at the Peninsula Campaign in Richmond and the Battle of Antietam in 1862.

McClellan ran on a "peace at any price" platform, not without some appeal to a nation riven by the Civil War. But it also gave Lincoln an opportunity. Lincoln selected Andrew Johnson as his running mate. Frank Coburn, of the Abraham Lincoln Museum in Harrogate, Tennessee, explains the significance of this choice, citing Mark Neely's book *The Abraham Lincoln Encyclopedia,* as his main source:

> "The nomination of General McClellan united the Republicans behind Lincoln. Seeking to appeal across partisan lines, the Republicans chose Andrew Johnson as Lincoln's running mate. At the start of the war, Johnson was a senator from Tennessee. He was the only senator from a seceding state that did not resign his seat. Lincoln named him War Governor of Tennessee. He was a 'War' Democrat, or a Democrat who followed Lincoln's war aims.

"On the other hand, Peace Democrats sought a convention of the states to settle their differences. Three days before the Republicans' nominating convention, Ward Hill Lamon, a Lincoln confidant, told John Hay, Lincoln's secretary, that he thought 'Lincoln rather prefers Johnson or some other War Democrat as calculated to give more strength to the ticket.' "

Neely believes that the decision to nominate Johnson was Lincoln's, but some historians have argued that Lincoln merely acceded to the wishes of the delegates. Without a doubt, a major factor in the equation was simply the political gain that could be exploited, as Thomas F. Schwartz, state historian at the Illinois Historic Preservation Agency, explains:

"Lincoln had hopes of building a viable Republican party within the reconstructed Southern states. Having a War Democrat on the ticket would also attract the votes of other War Democrats. George B. McClellan was seen by some in the Democratic Party as too conciliatory and willing to accept peace over reunifying the country."

In order to attract the most possible voters to the fold, the Republicans ran Lincoln under the name "National Union Party." As Coburn points out,

"This was done perhaps to imply that the Democrats were, by contrast, Dis-unionist. The selection of Andrew Johnson, both a War Democrat and a Southerner, promoted this image of the Union Party."

Of course, this Union Party also symbolized the spirit of reconciliation that Lincoln hoped to achieve after the War, and one of his rationales for the embrace of previous "enemies" might have been a conscious attempt to serve as a model for post–Civil War America.

Regardless of Lincoln's motives, the strategy worked, as the Republican National Committee's Gene Ulm is more than proud to point out:

David Feldman

"Loyalist border state Democrats flocked to the ticket. The Lincoln-Johnson Union Party, who advocated the abolition of slavery and the restoration of the union, were victorious over Democratic candidate General George B. McClellan by a substantial majority."

Submitted by Daniel A. Papcke of Lakewood, Ohio.

How Did the Police Determine the Speed of Drivers Before Radar Was Invented? How Do They Measure Speed in Localities Where Radar Isn't Allowed?

As long as there have been drivers, there have been drivers who are driving too fast. And for just as long as there have been drivers who are driving too fast, there have been police officers trying to prevent drivers from driving too fast. Indeed, speed limits have been part of the American fabric since at least June 12, 1652, when New Amsterdam (now New York City) enforced a law prohibiting the riding or driving of horses at a gallop within city limits.

Brian Traynor, of the U.S. Department of Transportation's Office of Enforcement and Emergency Services, was kind enough to provide *Imponderables* with a colorful time line of speed enforcement in the twentieth century.

Hartford, Connecticut, lays claim to the distinction of imposing the first speed limit in the U.S.—an 8 mph limit in the city and 12 mph in the "country" (suburbs). Once the notion of speed limits spread across the country, localities tried their hardest to invent

David Feldman

methods to ensure their measurement of speed was precise. For when Hartford's law was imposed, the only pursuit vehicle available to law enforcement was the bicycle. An officer on a bicycle was quite capable of nabbing the flagrant lawbreaker found careening around the city at, say, 10 mph, but was ill-equipped to nab those burning rubber at 40 mph.

Westchester County, New York, therefore, decided that trying to chase down a speeding car on a bicycle probably wasn't the most efficient way of solving the problem, so it introduced the stopwatch as a means of measuring the average speed of a car between fixed points. Over the next few decades, different technologies would be used to calculate the rates: slide rules; preprinted look-up tables; and eventually, calculators.

Traynor reports a particularly colorful "speed trap" that was quite advanced for its era:

> "New York City Commissioner William McAdoo set up a series of three dummy tree trunks at one-mile intervals along the Hudson Drive. A police officer equipped with a stopwatch and a telephone was concealed inside each fake tree. When a car sped past the first station, the officer inside telephoned the exact time to the officer in the next tree. The second officer set his watch accordingly. When the car passed his post, he computed its speed for the mile. If the speed was above the limit, he telephoned the officer in the third tree, who lowered a pole across the road and stopped the car."

Foiled by foliage!

Pity poor William Buxton. He was the first driver found guilty of speeding because of the high-tech device introduced in 1910: the "Photo-Speed Recorder." This contraption combined a camera synchronized with a stopwatch and operated by taking pictures of a speeding car at set times.

Other devices were created primarily for speed measurement purposes rather than for enforcement. David Hensing, deputy executive director of the American Association of State Highway and Transportation Officials, told *Imponderables* that the enoscope, invented by William Phelps Eno in the 1920s, consisting of two periscopes located at a known distance from each other, was a highly accurate gauge. And those mysterious air hoses that we drive over from time to time are usually used to measure speed for research purposes. They, too, are highly accurate, but are generally not used to nab speeders, partly because, according to Hensing, "many drivers discern [that] two hoses over the roadway are a speed measuring device rather than simply a counting device."

Law enforcement agencies started utilizing radar for speed citations after World War II, but at first the technology was almost as cumbersome as the "triple tree" strategy. Traynor reports:

> "Radar then used a graph as the permanent record of the speed reading. The radar unit was so heavy that a tripod or some mounting device was needed to hold it and the penscriber (graph printer); a station wagon was the usual transport-setup vehicle. Stops were usually made by calling the speed reading down the road (they had radios then) to a stop unit(s) or to chase officers at the setup site."

What we did not realize until we spoke to quite a few traffic officials is that radar and even fixed-point calculations without radar were never the dominant mode of catching speeders. "Pacing" was. And still is.

The classic "radar speed trap" has been banned in California, so pacing is particularly important. If a law enforcement official sees a vehicle cruising at excessive speeds, the "pacing car" lies behind the offending vehicle and attempts to maintain the same speed. Unmarked police cars can sometimes stay alongside the car for long stretches without detection. Greg Manuel, commander of public affairs for the California Highway Patrol, told *Imponderables* that pacing is the easiest, most reliable, and most efficient means of nabbing speeders. How can an offender explain away an officer in court testifying to the fact that a 70 mph pace in a 55 mph zone had been maintained for one and a half miles? About the only possible defense is that the officer's speedometer is broken. But the California Highway Patrol makes sure that speedometers are calibrated on a regular basis, usually once a year. So if the last calibration report confirms that the speedometer is "off" by one mph, the judge might knock off one mph from the charge.

California and many other states that don't rely on radar use aircraft to detect speeders. Officers walk off a designated area with measuring tape and mark it with painted stripes, often at quarter-mile intervals. Airborne officers track the movement of speeders between these stripes, and then contact cruisers stationed down-stream from the marked section. Even states that ban "speed traps" often allow airborne speed detection, and usually go out of their way to give a warning to potential miscreants, as David Hensing explains:

> "Signs are frequently posted indicating speed limits are enforced from the air, and some states use airplane-shaped painted markings in lieu of a plain stripe to remind motorists of this possibility."

These signs act as a deterrent, and might slow drivers as effectively as positioning marked patrol cars in the area.

Finally, we present the lowest-tech answer to detecting speed in the past and the present: In most localities, judges will accept a law enforcement officer's visual estimation of the speed of a vehicle. Greg Manuel claims that an experienced California Highway Patrol officer can estimate the speed of a vehicle within a few miles per hour.

Submitted by Ed Booth of Chico, California.

What Causes the Strong, Rather Unpleasant Smell Inside of New Refrigerators?

❧ "That's easy," replied Tracy Haak of the Association of Home Appliance Manufacturers. "I asked the engineering department and they replied, 'All the line workers put their old shoes in the refrigerators.' " But we knew she was kidding. We're not *quite* as dumb as we look.

We can think of two major purchases that, once brought back home, emit strong smells. One is the ineffable fragrance we call "new-car smell." In *Do Penguins Have Knees?*, we learned that "new-car smell" consisted of many ingredients, including paint, plastic, carpeting, upholstery fabric, vinyl, rubber, adhesives, and sealers.

Alas, the main culprit in the altogether less pleasant "new-fridge smell" is the same enemy that plagued Benjamin Braddock in *The Graduate:* plastics. J. Benjamin Horvay, a consulting engineer who specializes in residential refrigerators and food freezers, explains:

> "As a new refrigerator progresses down the assembly line, holes are drilled into the plastic food liner and inner door, shelf supports are snapped into place, and parts are assembled.
>
> "When the plastic material is thus penetrated, it gives up an odor that quickly dissipates under normal conditions. If, however, the door is closed and the cabinet is packaged before this can take place, the customer will notice the smell when he or she opens the door.
>
> "Added sources of odor might be the packaging materials, tapes that hold accessories in place, the vinyl door gasket, etc. Elevated temperatures during shipment would accentuate the bad odors."

Is there a high-tech solution to the problem? Nope. But there's a well-worn low-tech remedy. Horvay suggests that

> "once the cabinet is aired out and the inside is cooled down, the odors should disappear. An open box of baking soda, placed on a shelf, will expedite the process."

Submitted by Chesley Palmore of Tyler, Texas.

David Feldman

Why Does Root Beer Generate More Foam Than Colas or Other Soft Drinks? Why Is Root Beer the Only Carbonated Soft Drink That Seems to Retain Its Head Indefinitely? Does Root Beer Generate So Much Foam for the Same Reason That Alcoholic Beer Does?

Traditionally, as its name implies, root beer was flavored by extracts from the roots and bark of plants, most commonly sassafras. The foam associated with root beer is linked inextricably to proteins in the product. According to Brendan Gaffney, senior research specialist at Pepsi-Cola, makers of Mug root beer,

> "Protein stretches in contact with surfaces such as water, air and other contact surfaces to form films under turbulent conditions (shaking, pouring, pressure, etc.) that produce foam bubbles."

The same sassafras that traditionally provided the flavoring for root beer also tended to produce and preserve the foam (so did the birch in birch beer).

But about thirty years ago, the U.S. Food and Drug Administration ruled that sassafras was a carcinogen, and soft-drink producers scrambled to find substitutes, natural and chemical. Anthony Meushaw, executive director of the Society of Soft Drink Technologists, told *Imponderables* that when the FDA ruling was issued, some soft drink producers chose to shift to artificial flavorings but wanted to retain the distinctive "head" that has been responsible for many a foam mustache on children. So some companies chose to introduce artificial, chemical "foaming agents" that did not add to the taste of the drink—their sole purpose was to make sure that a head was formed and retained.

But many of the most popular root beers use natural foaming agents instead. For example, Pepsi's Mug root beer includes yucca and quallaia (a tree found in the Andes Mountains of Chile) extracts that are natural protein emulsions. But the slightly bitter taste of these plants is overpowered by the vanilla flavor in Mug: If it weren't for the foaming properties of the proteins in these plants, they probably would not be included, according to Gaffney.

Root beer became popular in the 1840s, long before the invention of colas. Presumably, the "beer" in root beer derived from the carbonation and head of the soft drink, and from the fact that some of the ancestors of root beer contained alcohol. Beer takes advantage of the natural proteins in rice and barley to retain its head. As you pour beer (or root beer) into the glass, the "shock" stretches the proteins and forms a head. Barring artificial foaming agents, the more protein in a drink, the higher and longer the foam is likely to form. By this measurement, then, Guinness Stout must have as much protein as a filet mignon.

Submitted by Bob Foreback of Ann Arbor, Michigan. Thanks also to Chuck Flagg of Houston, Texas, and Jim Wright of Cordele, Georgia.

David Feldman

Why Are You Supposed to Take Penicillin on an Empty Stomach?

❦ Our correspondent, Stephanie Lucas, wonders why, when most medications are prescribed to be taken with or after meals, penicillin is an exception. The answer is simple. Sort of.

Penicillin degrades easily in the presence of acid. And as Naomi Kaminsky, scientific affairs program manager of the American Pharmaceutical Association, explains,

> "Because the stomach makes acid when digesting food, taking penicillin with food breaks the medication up more quickly and less of it stays around long enough to be absorbed. On an empty stomach the pH is higher (more basic rather than more acid), so more of the medication is absorbed."

But if you think you must take penicillin on an empty stomach, Ron Cohen, pharmacist at the Philadelphia Pharmacy, recommends asking your doctor if it is truly necessary. The no-food indication developed when the earlier penicillin G was usually prescribed. Cohen says that patients were told not to eat one-half to one hour before or two hours after taking the drug. But about twenty years ago, penicillin VK was developed, which is more acid-stable. Penicillin VK has all but replaced penicillin G on prescription pads (one pharmacist we spoke to said, "This pharmacy currently has no doctors that use penicillin G"). VK promises faster onset of benefits to the body than penicillin G, and boasts the added bonus of not necessarily turning your need for an antibiotic into a three-hour fast.

Submitted by Stephanie Lucas of Vienna, Virginia.

Why Is There a Pink Stripe on the Left Side of Many Magazine Labels?

Two different representatives of the United States Postal Service replied: The pink stripe indicates that the magazine was sent second-class.

Simple, huh? Not quite so simple, actually.

We contacted one of our favorite sources, the folks at Neodata, a huge fulfillment house for magazine processing. When you subscribe to a magazine and send your check to Boulder, Colorado, or send your change of address to Boulder for a magazine based on the other side of the country, chances are you are sending your money to Neodata. Along with his colleagues, Chuck Vanstrom and Rob Farson, Biff Bilstein, vice president of sales, unleashed the sad saga of the pink stripe, and why pink is more prevalent on magazine labels today than it was years ago:

"A while ago the USPS gave preferential handling and delivery to 'time-dated' magazines such as dailies and weeklies. Since the publications were transported through the Postal System in canvas mail bags, the delivery routing tag on each bag was color coded to indicate this 'expeditious routing': red

David Feldman

(or actually, pink) for 'time-dated' publications; and buff for non-time-dated publications.

"However, once the magazine arrived at the 'destination' or the post office of the mail carrier, the magazines were removed from the canvas mail bag, and there was no longer any way to distinguish time-dated from non-time-dated publications. The U.S. Postal System then allowed time-dated publications to have a pink stripe on the label affixed to the publication.

"Subsequently, non-time-dated publishers objected to the perceived preferential handling associated with the pink-striped label. The USPS agreed with the position taken by these non-time-dated publishers, and allowed them to have a pink stripe on their label, also.

"So now every magazine wants the pink stripe on their label, for fear that without the stripe their magazine won't get preferential handling and delivery."

In other words, all second-class mailers seem to want first-class treatment.

Submitted by Jim Ellwanger of Tampa, Florida.

Pigs! This fashion season... **Think Pink!** At newsstands and feed stores near you!

OINQUE MONTHLY

That Pink Look!

All the news around the trough!

from silk purse publishers

Do Pigs Have Hair? If So, Do Pigs Have Pink Hair?

Although the pinkish, Porky Piggish pig that we know and love might appear to bare its epidermis to the world, we are left with two unalterable facts: All pigs are mammals; and all mammals have hair. Therefore, all pigs have hair. Indeed, if Patrick Stewart were a pig, he would have hair.

You can be forgiven if you didn't know that pigs have hair all over their bodies, for pigs' hair color matches the skin below. Kathleen Kovacs, *Imponderables'* trusted veterinarian (not that *we* go to her as patients), told us that a Chester White pig has white hair, and a Berkshire pig has both black and white hair, and that the pinkish Duroc pig does indeed have pink hair.

Submitted by Matthew Anderson of Haddon Township, New Jersey.

How in the World Were Marshmallows Invented?

❧ We don't think it will shock you to discover that marshmallows are not a natural substance. No, marshmallows don't grow on trees, vines, or underground.

But they weren't invented out of whole cloth, either. For there is a mallow plant, which, not coincidentally, tends to grow on marshes. The first culture that we know to have eaten the mallow plant was ancient Egypt, long before the reign of Cleopatra. Egyptians dried and pulverized the plant and considered it a delicacy.

But marshmallows as we know them weren't possible until someone came up with the idea of combining the mallow plant with sugar, and it was almost certainly an accident. Sugar's first use was as a way of making medicines more palatable, but a recurring problem was the tendency of sugar to crystallize. In India, they solved the problem by using gum arabic, but some countries did not have access to this form of gum. When boiled in hot water, the ground roots of the mallow plant turned out to be an effective gum. Combined with sugar, the first marshmallow was born.

The French were the first to turn marshmallows into a confection for the masses. Kraft Foods supplied a report researched by the Marshmallow Research Foundation (there *is* a foundation or association for just about anything):

> "The marshmallow in its present fluffy form originated in France and was known as *Pâté de Guimauve*. As made in the early nineteenth century, it contained the extract of the marshmallow root, dried and reduced to a powder. A light cream in color, the genuine marshmallow base contained starch, sugar, pectin, asparagine and a substance allied to lecithin.
>
> "The original marshmallow formula called for the following proportions—five pounds powdered marshmallow root, 50 pounds ground sugar, 30 pounds ground gum arabic, 60 pounds orange flower water and 70 or more egg whites. Euro-

pean manufacturers of medicinal confectionery still use this formula. However, because marshmallow root reputedly possessed medicinal properties, it was early abandoned by confectioners as a necessary marshmallow ingredient."

Mallow trees were naturalized in the salt marshes of the United States not long after they were introduced in Europe. At first, mallow root was used, but later was abandoned in order to save money, and replaced by a combination of gum arabic and egg white.

Today, you can buy big marshmallows, little marshmallows, chocolate marshmallows, and coconut marshmallows. But you can't find a marshmallow with mallow in it. We are left in the strange situation of eating a product that is named after an ingredient that is no longer in it.

Submitted by Deb Buschur of Indianapolis, Indiana.

Is It True That the Fifth Digit of a Social Security Number Is Always Even?

Ever since we received this question, we've been wowing folks with our "psychic" powers. When a party gets a little dull, we whip out our Carnac uniform, close our eyes as if conjuring up all our metaphysical energy, and announce to the assembled throng: "You all have an even-numbered fifth Social Security number."

Carnac is almost always right. Although the revelers never have actually expressed their amazement at our abilities, we have to assume that they are too overcome to express their awe. For the party always seems to break up soon thereafter.

We cannot tell a lie. In *When Do Fish Sleep?*, we already discussed the meaning of the digits in Social Security numbers, and we included this summary:

"Under the current system, the first three digits of a Social Security number indicate the state of residence of the holder at the time the number was issued. The remaining digits have no special meaning."

But even as we wrote those words, we remember thinking—what about that pesky hyphen? If the serial numbers are meaningless, why bother with the little hyphen after the fifth digit? The sixth through ninth numbers, which the SSA refer to as "serial numbers," are truly, according to the agency's own procedures bulletin, "a straight numerical series of numbers from 0001 to 9999 within each group."

But the two middle digits are called a "group number." Although these two digits have no specific geographic or data significance, according to the Social Security Bulletin,

"[They are] used to break the numbers into blocks of convenient size for SSA's processing operations and for controlling the assignments to the States."

But if the numbers don't have a special meaning, why do an overwhelming majority of Americans have even-numbered fifth digits? We were frustrated when we discovered that one of the first people we contacted at the SSA, associate commissioner for public affairs Trish Butler, responded:

"It is not true that the fifth digit of your SSN is always even. In fact, the fifth digit of my SSN is five."

But there is a strange pattern to the assignment of the group numbers. SSA regional public affairs officer John Clark explains the arcane procedure:

"For each area (the first three digits) the group number (middle two digits) follows a particular sequence designed to discourage outsiders from thinking about it. The group sequence begins with odd numbers 01 through 09, then goes through even numbers 10 through 96, then even numbers 02 to 08, and finally odd numbers 11 to 99."

Why bother with this tortuous system? The answer lies in that "designed to discourage outsiders from thinking about it" part of the statement. Although we couldn't get Clark to amplify the suggestive comment, another SSA source, off the record, indicated that the group number can sometimes help nab forgers who don't understand the code.

If a fifty-year-old bears an odd fifth digit, the jig is up, because before 1965, the only odd fifth digits issued were 01, 03, 05, 07, and 09. No more odd fifth digits were originated until numbers 10 through 96 were exhausted. And *this* is why all but the youngest Americans will have even five-digit SSNs—unless their fourth number is zero.

So the Carnac routine will work more often than not. Just remember: If your subject says that his or her fifth digit is odd, wow them with the offhand observation that it is preceded by a zero. You can break up a party just as deftly as we do.

Submitted by Dan Hughes of Urbana, Illinois. Thanks also to Maureen Chen of Flushing, New York.

$\mathcal{W}hy$ Is There No Period After the Second "S" in S.O.S Pads? How Did the Pads Get Their Unusual Name?

☞ S.O.S pads were invented in 1917 by Erwin W. Cox, a door-to-door salesman who sold aluminum pots and pans. Cox produced his pads by hand-dipping them in soap in his own basement. Originally, his motive in creating the pads was merely to make sure his cookware sparkled so that customers would be more likely to buy them.

Little did he realize that the demand for his soap pads would far outstrip that for his cooking utensils. In order to line up sufficient financing, Cox was forced to subdivide and sell his patent rights on a geographical basis. In 1919, a California company was formed to sell the products in the western eleven states. Cox left his San Francisco home and established a midwestern base, the S.O.S Company, with a Chicago factory, while another group concentrated on the eastern portion of the United States.

How did he come up with the name of his product? One source we contacted at S.O.S says that Mrs. Cox is often given credit for the name, which she considered appropriate because "it is the universal call for help and it also is the first letters of 'Save Our Saucepans.' " Erwin Cox applied for a trademark for "S.O.S" but was denied because the abbreviation duplicated the internationally recognized distress signal. By eliminating the last period, as a current S.O.S spokesperson told *Imponderables,* Cox satisfied trademark requirements and was left with a subtle difference that is "noted only by the most astute observers."

In the early 1920s, the western contingent bought out Cox and consolidated the entire business in Chicago, and eventually the business has gone through the ownership of three large corporations: General Foods; Miles Laboratories; and S.O.S's current parent, Clorox Company.

Submitted by Myrton Giles of Homewood, Illinois.

Why Do Some Baseball Bats Have a Black Stripe Around Them?

This Imponderable was first posed by a fan of Jim Eason's talk-fest on KGO-AM in San Francisco. The caller assumed that the band was the trademark of a particular company bat, but other folks chimed in with their theories. One mentioned that he thought it marked the sweet spot of the bat. Another caller claimed that it designated the pine-tar line (the point at which pine tar could no longer be applied to the handle of a bat). We opined that perhaps it was an obscure fashion statement that we nonjocks, with our dweebish sense of aesthetics, just couldn't understand.

Alas, it turns out that the thin black stripe is a sort of Forrest Gump of modern baseball history, a minor "player" in some of the changes in baseball over the last half-century. The initial caller had it right: The black stripe is a trademark of Adirondack, a bat manufacturer now owned by sporting equipment giant Rawlings.

Before it was bought out by Rawlings in 1975, Adirondack had been making bats independently since the 1940s. For most of that time, Adirondack bats were stripeless. But that changed when

Frank Torre, brother of player-manager Joe Torre, obtained a job with the company; Torre was hired as a "pro-rep," with the responsibility of trying to sell pro players on using Adirondack bats.

Luckily for him, Frank was a former teammate of The Hammer, Henry Aaron. He extracted a promise from Aaron to at least try the brand in some games. According to Bill Steele, master batmaker at Adirondack, Torre wanted to know if Aaron was keeping his promise. So Frank Torre thought of the idea of putting a distinctive mark, a stripe, down the middle of the bat. Torre figured that the stripe was distinctive enough so that he could tell from his vantage point in the stands at a stadium, or at home on television, whether Hammerin' Hank was living up to his end of the bargain. At one point, only Aaron had a stripe on his Adirondack bat. Aaron used his Adirondacks intermittently, but he did knock his historic 500th homer with an Adirondack.

The powers that be at Adirondack realized the marketing possibilities of a trademarked design element (after all, Louisville Slugger, number one in the bat business, always emblazoned their bats with a distinctive insignia). They dubbed the stripe the "Pro-Ring."

Over the years, the stripe has changed almost as often as hemlines on women's skirts. What began as a thin stripe grew at one point to approximately three inches wide. The basic black stripe metamorphosed into "designer colors." According to Tim Socha, of Rawlings-Adirondack marketing, each team has all its Adirondack users sport the same-colored stripe. Although black and navy blue remain the most popular colors, Adirondack has created other color combinations, including dark-colored bats with light-colored rings. The stripe remains in the same place for all teams; although it may look like the stripe bisects the length of the bat, it is actually a little closer to the handle than the meat end.

Socha mentioned that over the past fifteen years or so, the logos of bat manufacturers have grown larger and larger, presumably in order to snare free product plugs on television. Not only did the stripe around the bat get wider, but the script "Rawlings" and block-letter "Adirondack" became more prominent as well.

Eventually, Major League Baseball clamped down on this commercialism and ordered bat companies to downsize logos. Rawlings relented, reducing the width of the stripe to its current mere three-quarters of an inch, and reducing the size of the company name. As part of this compliance, Adirondack no longer paints the Pro-Ring 360 degrees around the bat, stopping short of intersecting the company name.

Rawlings-Adirondack calls their professional line of bats the "Big Stick." Each major league player who uses Adirondacks receives personalized treatment. On the meat end of each bat, the player's name and team are listed. So if Henry Aaron were playing for Atlanta today, the bat would read: "Big Stick—Aaron—Braves." This line is printed 90 degrees from the side of the bat where the batter should make contact (i.e., the label should be "faceup" at the point where the hitter makes contact). If the label is facing up, it ensures that the desirable smooth grain contacts the ball. If you see the ball hit the Pro-Ring, chances are you're looking at a very good pitcher, a very bad hitter, or a broken bat. Or all three.

Submitted by a caller on "The Jim Eason Show," San Francisco, California.

How Do Canning Companies Peel Off the Whitish Membranes of Mandarin Oranges Without Mutilating Them?

The traditional Japanese method of removing membranes is, to say the least, labor-intensive. Unpeeled mandarins are passed through a steam or hot-water bath for about one minute, which makes them easier to peel, and then cooled in cold water.

The fruit is then peeled by hand and set on trays to dry. Human hands are also responsible for separating the sections. Once sectioned, the fruit is placed in a solution of 2.5 percent hydrochloric acid for approximately two hours to remove those stringy fibers that are especially tough on mandarin oranges. After the hydrochloric bath, the sections are dipped into a 1 percent solution of sodium hydroxide to remove any remaining acid, and are then washed in pure water again before being canned.

Catherine Clay, public information specialist at the state of

David Feldman

Florida Department of Citrus, who provided us with much of the information in this chapter, wanted us to warn *Imponderables* readers, "Don't try this at home!" Both sodium hydroxide and hydrochloric acid can be extremely caustic. And on a more practical level, mandarin oranges are delicate. It would be difficult to apply these processes yourself without bruising the fruit.

The USDA has recently approved a new method for canning fresh citrus. By injecting citrus with pectinase, a group of naturally occurring enzymes usually derived from apples, the peel of citrus can be easily vacuum-suctioned from even heavier citrus, including oranges and grapefruits.

Submitted by Cynthia Lynn of White River Junction, Vermont.

In Marching Bands, Why Are Woodwinds Placed Behind the Brass? Wouldn't They Be Drowned Out by the Louder Brass?

☞ Good question, Jennifer, for you have exposed one of the nasty little secrets about marching bands. Not only are woodwinds drowned out by brass in front of them, they would be drowned out by brass behind them. Alas, we are sad to report that like sleazy film directors who seek budding ingenues in Hollywood, band directors want woodwind players primarily for their bodies, as Paul Droste, past president of the North American Brass Band Association, explains:

> "It is almost impossible to get concert hall balance with any great volume of sound on the football field. Even with a large woodwind section, its projection outdoors is almost negligible. Most bands treat the woodwind players as additional bodies for drill and formation; therefore, it is not important where to place them on the football field.
>
> "Music arrangers often write 'filler' or 'doubling parts' for the woodwinds, rather than independent parts of importance. The brass and percussion sections are featured; therefore they

are placed . . . closer to the audience. Some all-brass marching bands—and drum and bugle corps—do not use woodwinds at all."

Droste himself was the former director of a woodwindless ensemble, the all-brass and percussion Ohio State University Marching Band.

We spoke to David Henning, director of the University of Iowa Marching Band, who echoed all of Droste's explanations. Henning stresses that in a football venue, sheer volume is of great importance—having the brass front the band makes sense when the music is competing for attention with crowd noise and vast open spaces.

Despite the supremacy of brass over the more delicate woodwinds in marching bands, there is a movement afoot to give woodwinds a more prominent role. According to Henning, although the woodwinds may not be audible to many listeners, they provide "added tone color" that can make bands sound better. The University of Iowa's marching band is huge (260 pieces) and has a distinctive sound because it incorporates twenty-four piccolos. Henning reports that other bands, especially high schools, who play in smaller venues, are starting to feature woodwinds more prominently. Arrangements are written that will occasionally feature only the woodwinds and percussion, enabling the woodwind players to feel that they are more than a drill team with sticks in their hands.

Submitted by Jennifer Martz of Phoenixville, Pennsylvania.

Why Is the Holiday Called "Good" Friday When It Commemorates the Crucifixion of Jesus?

⌘ This Imponderable was posed by a lay Sunday school teacher who has always wondered about the strange name of this somber day. Could, he wondered, have the "Good" been ironic?

One expert, Erroll F. Rhodes, an assistant director at the American Bible Society, indicates that such an interpretation is possible. But he, like all of the other sources we contacted, was more inclined to see the "Good" as a demonstration of Christian faith:

"One settles on the rhetorical level by calling it an example of irony. Another [rationale] is based on a recognition that humanity was redeemed through the supreme sacrifice of Christ on the cross. Superficially, this may be described as a paradox, but theologians have traditionally called it a mystery, recognizing that without Good Friday there can be no Easter—a profound truth of experience that (in the words of Mark Twain) is stranger than fiction."

It might be difficult for non-Christians to comprehend how believers could not see the anniversary of their Savior as a day to be mourned rather than celebrated. But from the religious perspective, many "tragedies" are perceived through the prism of later redemption. Marie Anne Mayeskie, of Loyola Marymount University's department of theology, eloquently expresses this point of view:

"Good Friday is called 'Good' because it is the day on which Christians celebrate the accomplishment of salvation by Christ. It is, in Christian liturgical celebration particularly, not essentially a sad, though certainly a solemn event, which is viewed from the perspective of the Resurrection. The Christian tradition understands the work of Christ to have transformed the human realities of death, and even sin.

"In this connection, a solemn prayer for the Easter Vigil calls the sin of Adam 'a happy fault which merited so great a redeemer.' "

Submitted by Ed Swanson of Santa Monica, California.

TRY OVR ANCIENT FORMVLA

FEAR NOT GRAY HAIR SIR...

IN 16 OZ. OR 32 OZ. VRNS

How Does Grecian Formula Know What Color to Make Your Hair? How Does It Take Out the Gray Without Changing the Natural Color of the Hair?

❧ Scan the hair-coloring section of the local cosmetics emporium, and you'll find scores of different color choices. But Grecian Formula promises to take out gray from any colored hair and restore it to its natural color—there are no separate Grecian Formulas for blond hair and black hair.

How does Grecian Formula work? The protein in hair contains a natural brownish-black pigment called melanin. Dark hair has more melanin than light hair. As we age, the melanin levels decrease, and gray hair appears. Grecian Formula, applied in small doses on a daily basis, deposits thin layers of color inside and outside of the hair shaft. Each daily application of Grecian Formula is quite small, so it might take weeks to achieve the appropriate color (usually, approximately three weeks to produce a medium-brown color). Once the proper hair color has been attained, a reapplication of Grecian Formula might be required only once or twice a week.

But how can the same product re-create pale-blond hair and jet-

David Feldman

black hair in the process of removing the gray? To find the answer, we spoke to Dr. Herbert Lapidus, vice president of research and development at Combe Incorporated, the manufacturers of Grecian Formula. He informed us that Grecian Formula doesn't really "know" what the natural color of the user was; it doesn't even "care." For the melanin in blond hair is exactly the same color as the melanin in black hair—there is just much less of it. An albino has no melanin in his skin; Africans have far more than whites or Asians. Blond hair contains the same color of melanin as black hair, so Grecian Formula will work just as effectively on it as black hair. But fewer layers of Grecian Formula are necessary to color light hair. If a blonde wanted darker hair, extra applications of Grecian Formula will do the trick.

Submitted by Charles Myers of Ronkonkoma, New York. Thanks also to Pete Weiss of Howell, Michigan, and George Gjelfriend of East Orlando, Maine.

Why Is Regular Chewing Gum Packaged in Foil but Bubble Gum Packaged in Wax Paper?

Traditionally, bubble gum was sold only in individual pieces and was wrapped in wax paper. Wax doesn't protect the gum as well as foil, but since the bubble gum was presumably an impulse purchase imminently to be turned into a mastication vehicle, the bubble gum would retain its freshness.

According to Tim Boyle, corporate spokesperson for Topps, the manufacturer of the best-selling individual-sized bubble gum brand, Bazooka, the wax paper is retained for tradition's sake in all of its "chunk" sizes: "The wax has a fairly long shelf life—certainly long enough for this quick-turnover item." Boyle admitted that wax wrapping costs less than foil, but assured us that if the gum required foil to extend its shelf life, Topps would use it.

Multipiece gum of any kind, including bubble gum, tends to have an overwrap of foil. Bubble Yum, for example, uses foil to wrap the five pieces in the package, but the individual pieces have a wax wrap. A product manager from Planters Life Savers, who wished to remain anonymous, told *Imponderables* that the outer foil is sufficient to keep the gum moist.

Nonbubble chewing gum, which has always been sold primarily in multipacks, uses foil not only to extend shelf life but to assure freshness after the package has been opened by the consumer.

Submitted by Johanna Doerr of Chalfont, Pennsylvania.

Why Are the Numbers 1 Through 12 Printed on the Wrappers of a Burger King Whopper?

Burger King's Teresa McNally was happy to lead us through the mystery of the Whopper numbers. Actually, the same digits appear on all BK sandwiches, not just burgers, and they are all printed for the same reason: to make sure that the sandwiches are fresh.

As you might have guessed, the numbers correspond to the numbers on an analog clock. After a sandwich is cooked and wrapped, one of the twelve numbers is slashed with a nontoxic grease pencil. But the slash refers not to the *hour* at which the burger was cooked, but to where the *minute* hand of the clock is at the point the sandwich is wrapped. For example, if a hamburger with cheese is wrapped at ten minutes after the hour, the "2" is marked (because the minute hand has just hit the 2).

Burger King's policy is to allow a sandwich to sit out for a maximum of ten minutes. So any sandwiches left in the bins are discarded (in our example, the burger would be thrown away after the minute hand reached the 4).

Of course, Burger King has long attempted to distinguish itself from other fast-food franchises by allowing the customer to have their burgers "your way." During peak periods (in most locations, peak is lunchtime hours, from noon until two), sandwiches are prepared continuously and will be sold to customers within a minute or two. During nonpeak periods, food is prepared virtually to order, based on previous sales demand at that hour, but a few of the most popular sandwiches are prepared in advance in order to expedite service.

French fries are even more subject to deterioration of freshness than sandwiches. Burger King's policy is to toss fries that have been sitting for seven minutes. But, alas, the french fry package is numberless.

Submitted by Catherine Jackson of Katy, Texas.

$\mathcal{D}oe\mathcal{S}$ the Military Mandate a Particular Arrangement of Browns and Greens in the Design of Camouflage? Or Is It Random?

✎ One look at military camouflage would lead one to believe that the patterns are as random as a painting at the Museum of Modern Art. But take a second look. More than a few folks make a living figuring out how to arrange those blobs of color.

One historian at the U.S. Army Center of Military History scoffed at the notion that there was a prescribed pattern: "If it was standard, it wouldn't be camouflage." So how do strategists determine the patterns? The two most important variables in camouflage design are the shades of color and shapes to be included. Obviously, you need different colors to mask troops in the desert than in a forest. But almost as important as the color is the shape of the patterns, particularly crucial in disguising large objects, such as military vehicles.

We spoke to Terry Cummerford, a research chemist at Natick Research and Development Center, who tests camouflage for battle dress uniforms. Cummerford reports that the colors for camouflage are initially determined from soil samples and photographs.

Using a video camera and a field spectrometer, a terrain analysis instrument designed and patented by the military, researchers feed the color data into a computer. This analysis can be amazingly detailed, noting the color of leaves on trees and the varying shades of tree barks.

Specially formulated software then analyzes the terrain for up to five dominant colors and shapes. Depending upon the requests of the military, camouflage can be created with only two colors and four shapes or four colors and two shapes. More often, the military asks the computer to generate the design for many different camouflage samples and then field-tests the uniforms for detectability.

The U.S. Army currently uses two types of camouflage for standard-issue battle dress uniforms: woodland and desert. In arctic terrain, the military, reasonably enough, finds all-white uniforms to be the best camouflage.

The military usually creates its own designs for the camouflage of its vehicles. R. D. Thompson, program manager of Teledyne Engineering, told *Imponderables* that his company receives color and pattern specifications from the military and applies camouflage in a process not unlike the silk-screening of T-shirts. Surprisingly, the camouflage of large vehicles is usually hand-drawn. Unlike the blobby patterns of battle dress uniforms, most ship camouflage features jagged geometric patterns, simulating the angularity of waves in the ocean.

Submitted by Clarinda de Guzman of Rockville, Maryland. Thanks also to Dennis Kingsley of Goodrich, Michigan.

Why Do Two Cereal Flakes That Are Floating in Milk Tend to Float Toward Each Other Once They Get Less Than an Inch Apart?

Our initial attempts to find the answer to this intriguing Imponderable met with total frustration, until a kind soul, Diane Dickey of Kellogg's, took pity on us. Although she is in the communications department at the cereal giant, Dickey was carried away by the lure of quashing Imponderability. As she wrote in *The Kellogg's News:*

> "Our first instinct was to tell Feldman not to play with his food. However, because this question kept staring at us from the cereal bowl, we invited John Kepplinger from Product Research to accept the challenge of explaining why flakes do seem to attract each other in a bowl of milk."

Kepplinger then consulted with eight different Kellogg's experts, ranging from the divisions of Product Research, Food Research, and Technical Services. Kepplinger's summary of their conclusions was straightforward:

> "The primary explanation for why two cereal flakes attract each other in milk is due to surface tension. Surface tension causes the milk to form a small valley around each flake. As the two flakes move closer together, these valleys meet to form a natural depression between the flakes and they simply slide downhill toward each other."

But wanting to make sure that the answer was complete, Kepplinger contacted Philip A. Sorenson, vice president of Advanced Technology Innovations, Inc. Sorenson called Dr. Bob Park, director of public affairs with the American Physical Society. In a letter, Sorenson summarized Park's findings:

> "Using two leaves in a pond as our example, he [Park] said that the leaves essentially 'take a random walk around the pond' until they get close enough to one another. Each leaf is pressing on the surface of the water; this weight deforms the surface tension of the water around the leaf, and the surface of the water 'dips' if the leaves are close enough to one another, causing the leaves to effectively lean toward one another in this slight indentation.
>
> "To illustrate this point, Dr. Park said to picture stretched rubber, onto which two marbles are placed. Each marble

presses the surface of the rubber downwards, causing the marbles to roll toward one another . . ."

Another consultant that Sorenson contacted implied that the movement of the flakes might not be as random as Park suggested. So we consulted the physicists on the Usenet boards on the Internet, who proceeded to shower us with various other "randomizing elements" that can affect the movement of the two little flakes. Don Berkowitz, of Chesapeake College, mentioned that because both the average motion of the particles and surface tension are functions of temperature, the temperature of the milk would play a role. Others added that small air currents in the air, ripples from the spoon, sugar, or other coatings on the cereal could all affect the movement of the flakes.

Physicist Stan Berry, of Nichols Research Corp., reminded us that seemingly insignificant movements can alter the flakes' progress:

"Bumping the table could work as well as hitting your spoon on the bowl. Also, the cereal flakes would automatically retain some inherent motion as they are dropped into the bowl. On a slippery surface (such as milk) it takes great care to ensure that two things start out at rest relative to each other."

At the same time that we were weighing in with our cereal Imponderable, another similar question was embroiling the newsgroup: Why do tea leaves tend to congregate in the middle (and bottom) of a tea cup? The consensus was that when stirred, tea leaves group in the middle because of the lesser frictional force on the inside edge of the tea leaves (slower currents) than on the outside edge of the leaves (where the currents are swifter).

Physicist Andrew DeWeerd argued that surface tension might explain the bond between the flakes once they have joined, but that the initial attraction of cereal flakes might be explained by the same tendency to "meet in the middle" as the tea leaves. Noting that the pressures of stirring or pouring the milk will tend to drive the liquid either clockwise or counterclockwise, De Weerd writes:

"I would assume that these currents are maintained for quite some time. Since the currents on the outside of the flake (bowl side) are greater, you would have a push toward the middle. I would also suspect that the flake turns slowly about its center in the same angular direction as the milk in the bowl.

"Geez, this is a problem for the national labs to work on. Might solve the gyroscopic stability problem they are having with the Titans."

Unfortunately, despite the suggestion, *Imponderables* was unsuccessful in eliciting the interest of the military-industrial complex in solving the cereal riddle, but that doesn't mean that others haven't done experimental research; judging from the two contributions that follow, the United Kingdom seems to be the epicenter of cereal-attraction research. We received this report from Robert J. Hill, of Krisalis Software Ltd., who wanted to test whether if a cold bowl of milk was warmed slightly, convection would occur (i.e., heat rising from the edge of the bowl pushing the flakes together).

"I have tried this experiment on a prerefrigerated bowl of milk taken straight from the fridge, to which I added two flakes. They were moving around but not toward each other a great deal, so I placed my hands around the bowl. Within a couple of minutes the flakes joined. Maybe they would have joined without the heat from my hands, but I think we could be onto the major discovery of '95."

But we're afraid that we might have to award the "discovery of '95" prize to the U.K.'s Ian Russell, of Interactive Science, a group that organizes scientific exhibitions. He E-mailed us breathlessly, fresh from the thrill of revelation:

"I've just been down to the kitchen. No cornflakes available, but I can solemnly report that floating Rice Krispies like each other as well. [Could Crackle be responsible for this phenomenon? Maybe *this* is what he does for a living?]

David Feldman

"And you're *really* going to enjoy this: bits of hydrophobic [i.e., incapable of uniting with or absorbing water or liquid] candle-wax like each other as well. But they *don't* like hydrophilic [moisture-absorbent] Rice Krispies. They push each other apart. I suspect candle wax doesn't like cornflakes either.

Russell leaves us with the first physics poem ever published in an *Imponderables* book:

> Unlike poles attract; like poles repel.
> Unlike charges attract; like charges repel.
> Wax attracts wax.
> Cornflakes attract cornflakes.
> Wax repels cornflakes.
> Cornflakes repel wax.
> Isn't that interesting?

Er.

Submitted by Scott Wolber of Delmont, Pennsylvania.

SPECIAL THANKS to these technical experts at Kellogg's: Emery Okos; Jim Kincaid; Dean Baas; Jim Holder; John Richards; Jerry Ngeh-Ngwainbi; Dick Sherman; and Tammy Mitchell.

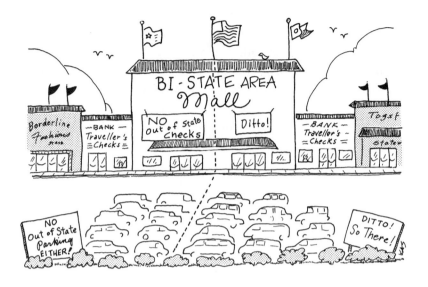

$\mathcal{W}hy$ Are Businesses Reluctant to Accept Out-of-State Checks When They'll Accept In-State Checks From Far-Flung Places?

❧ If stores weren't afraid of receiving bad checks, they wouldn't push credit-card sales, for which they must kick back a percentage to Visa or American Express. But bad checks are a perpetual problem. And in-state residents just aren't as likely to try to pass bad checks as "foreigners." Transients pass far more bad checks than locals, and tend to be oblivious about their credit ratings, but still: Transients can come from in state as well as out of state.

So we spoke to Nalini Rogers, senior financial analyst at the Federal Reserve Board in Washington, D.C. Rogers's theory is that the "discrimination" against out-of-state checks probably stems from Regulation CC, which determines how long banks can hold funds from checks. A bank is allowed to retain money longer for out-of-state checks than for local ones (actually, the Federal Reserve Board has divided the U.S. into forty-eight territories, many but not all of which are states).

So if you are a merchant in Sarasota, Florida, who receives a check from Urbandale, Iowa, your bank is entitled to withhold the funds for days longer, a killer to cash flow for the retailer. The justification for the rule is that the check cashed in Florida needs to "go back" and "return" from Iowa, lengthening the time that a bank needs to ascertain whether there are sufficient funds to cover the check. Of course, now the communication between the two banks is done electronically.

But in speaking to retailers, we heard constant kvetching about the difficulties involved in handling out-of-state checks. For one, local authorities will often not aid in the collection of bad checks from out of state. As Tucson, Arizona, Radio Shack manager Jed Peretz put it:

> "Is Arizona going to extradite a bad-check writer from California for a $150 check? I kind of doubt it."

Why do we get the feeling that Jed's question was not hypothetical? For he shared with us one example of how easy it is for a business to get burned by an out-of-state check:

> "We took a check from a customer from San Bernardino, California. He had a check-guarantee card from Bank of America and all the proper I.D. What we didn't know is that Bank of America in California discontinued its check-guarantee program and the check was worthless!"

Another store manager told *Imponderables* that his enterprising boss, suspicious about whether a local check would clear, once walked to the bank and cashed the check immediately. Good move. Just after he withdrew the money, the boss found the customer trying to close her account.

Submitted by Daniel Klein of North Bellmore, New York.

In Gift Boxes of Chocolate, Why Are Some Pieces Individually Wrapped in Their Own Foil While Others Are Unwrapped?

In our experience, when we have undertaken the arduous task of disassembling the foil from chocolates in gift assortments, we've been disappointed. The wrapped candies don't seem to be any better or more unusual than their naked, non-labor-intensive companions.

Most of our candy sources agreed with the two explanations provided by Robert J. Zedik, director of technical services for the National Confectioners Association:

> "The wrapping of individual chocolates in a boxed selection is basically for presentation. An occasional piece wrapped in brightly colored foil livens up the presentation of the entire assortment. However, some pieces having highly flavored centers might need to be individually wrapped to prevent the flavor from being absorbed by the other pieces in the box."

The most likely fragrance offenders are strong-smelling nutmeats, such as walnuts, or liquor-spiked candies.

We wondered whether a foil wrap could help preserve the shelf life of the candy. Ronald Z. Blankers, director of quality control for See's Candies, indicated that by reducing its exposure to oxygen and moisture, a wrap could extend shelf life. But there is no indication that foil-wrapped chocolates are any more perishable than the bare ones in the box, and most consumers are aware that fine chocolates are not expected to retain their freshness as long as a candy bar.

Indeed, both See's and Russell Stover no longer use foil wrap on any of their regular gift assortments, including the famous Whitman's Sampler (now marketed by Russell Stover). Brett Stone, director of retail for Russell Stover, told *Imponderables* that his company's only chocolate candy regularly wrapped in foil is the "Candy Jar Chocolate" line. But the foil's purpose isn't to preserve

David Feldman

the freshness of these candies, which are designed to lie uneaten longer than most assortments.

Stone reports that many manufacturers put on paraffin or confectioner's glaze to provide a sheen to the chocolate coating of their chocolate, but these additives lend an "off" taste (you can sample this taste in cheap chocolate-covered peanuts and raisins). Once again, the foil's purpose is to preserve the sheen of the coating, not extend shelf life.

Of course, in most households we know, any worry about the duration of shelf life of chocolates is a purely academic concern.

Submitted by Bonnie L. Cohen of Hamden, Connecticut.

Why Don't Cruise Controls on Automobiles Work on Speeds Below 30 mph?

From a technical point of view, there would be little trouble instituting cruise controls at lower speeds. But in practice, it wouldn't be used often and would almost certainly be dangerous.

Every time the brake pedal is depressed, cruise-control mechanisms are automatically disabled. When do drivers travel at speeds lower than 30 mph? In city stop-and-go traffic, of course. What good is using the cruise control if it goes off and on every few seconds?

Vann H. Wilber, director of the safety and international department of the American Automobile Manufacturers Association, which represents the Big Three automakers, explains the mechanism and the safety considerations:

> "All cruise-control systems have what is known as a low-speed cutoff. This cutoff is usually in the 25–30 mph speed range.

This intentional 'disabling' of a cruise control system at low speeds recognizes that low-speed traffic situations generally require a higher level of direct operator control over the vehicle and therefore the 'passive' throttle control of a cruise control system may not be appropriate under these conditions."

Submitted by Jeff Dehn of Hamilton, Illinois.

W*hy* Do Dogs Walk on Crooked Back Legs?

✎ As Homer Simpson is wont to say as he whacks his forehead with the palm of his hand, "Doh!" We can't believe that we walked into a sucker trap again.

Whenever we have a question about the "strange" anatomy of animals' feet or legs, we invariably forget the same lesson that we learned in *Do Penguins Have Knees?*: A knee is not always a knee. Nancy Purtill, of UCLA's biology department, was more than happy to chastise us:

> "If by 'crooked' you mean, why do dogs' knees point backward instead of forward, it's because that thing that looks like their knee is actually their ankle and they're walking on their toes."

OK, we'll admit it. That *is* what we meant. Nancy wasn't the only person to take us to task. Fred Lanting, a dog breeder and show judge, warned us sternly that if we were given an extra couple of extremities, ours would be "crooked" too:

....

D*avid* F*eldman*

"If *you* walked on all fours, you would also walk mostly on your fingers and toes, which is what most animals do, including dogs. The dog's foot is much longer in proportion to his lower leg (tibia/fibula) and upper thigh (femur). He stands on his rear toes so that the hock joint (ankle) and heel (hock or fibular tarsal bone where the Achilles' tendon is attached from the calf) is nearly one-third the way up to the hip joint from the ground.

We stand with about a ninety-degree angle between feet and legs, but the dog stands at between 110 to 160 degrees or so, so the dog's leg at that point is far less crooked or bent than humans' are."

Is there any advantage to the dog's conformation? Absolutely, according to Ithaca, New York, D.V.M. Robert Habel:

"The flexion of the joints allows for extension of the joints in the propulsion phase of the stride. The hind limbs provide most of the drive, while the forelimbs provide support. People have straight hind limbs most of the time, but visualize a human sprinter in the blocks waiting for the starter's shot. Are his or her hind legs crooked? You bet. You can't come from where you ain't been. . . ."

Such grammar from a Cornell University professor!

Another one of our dog experts, Lucille Kubichek, notes that the anatomy of dogs' legs assists them in jumping and leaping, as well:

"Compare the angles of dogs' back legs with a leap frog or kangaroo. The angle created by joints at the knee and heel, and the muscles attached to them, facilitate leaping.

"Some breeds have more angled back legs than others. The German shepherd or Alsatian, for example, have exaggerated angles in their back legs. A smooth fox terrier I once owned, whose back legs were not so angled, could, however, leap straight up vertically into my lap from a standing position.

"Spaniels often leap vertically in the field to see over brush and weeds when spotting birds during a hunt. Except for heavy dogs like St. Bernards, most dogs are excellent leapers."

Why Are There Always Holes in the Wafers of Ice Cream Sandwiches?

☙ We've tackled Imponderables about holes in doughnuts (*Why Do Clocks Run Clockwise?*) and bagels (*When Do Fish Sleep?*) in the past. But they were easy. Those have one hole apiece. With this training under our belt, we feel we are now qualified to discuss the mysterious origins of multi-hole foodstuffs.

Or more accurately, Samuel J. Nichols, marketing director for Quality Chekd Dairy Products Association, is qualified to answer:

> "The holes are called 'docker pin' holes, and are there for an even, consistent cooking process and therefore help maintain the consistency in both the cooking and cooling."

And what happens if that consistent temperature is not maintained? According to Ben Benjamin, director of development and quality assurance at Good Humor–Breyers Ice Cream, the wafers will warp. Even worse, if heat doesn't escape, Robert D. Byrne, director of product safety and technology at the International Dairy Food Association, warns, the holes "prevent them from blowing up during baking." And we're quite sure that ice cream sandwich manufacturers hate it when *that* happens.

Submitted by Diane Watterson of New Orleans, Louisiana. Thanks also to Jason Wallulis of Lebanon, Oregon.

Why Do Saltines Have Holes?

❧ Who better to answer this question than the company historian of Nabisco, David Stivers? The answer: same as the above, we're afraid. Saltines, especially, are so thin and light that without holes, the cracker would tend to cool unevenly, leaving the middle soft. Stivers reminded us that most crackers (including best-selling Ritz) have holes too, for the identical reason.

And we were saddened to learn that Nabisco has no cool nickname for the holes in its saltines. As far as we know, saltines don't blow up, either.

Submitted by Darin Marrs of Keller, Texas. Thanks also to Jacob Schneider of Norwalk, Ohio; Linda Burchfield of Birmingham, Alabama; and Leslie Alexander of Martin, North Dakota.

$\mathcal{W}hy$ Do the Winners of the Indianapolis 500 Drink Milk in Victory Lane?

❧ What would you want to do after winning a grueling 500-mile race? Stretch your legs? Visit the bathroom? Go to Disney World?

For more than fifty years, winning drivers at the Indianapolis Motor Speedway have been making the curious decision to cap their victory by guzzling milk. The originator of this custom was Louis Meyer, who first won the Indy 500 in 1928. When Meyer arrived back at the pits after his 1933 victory (back then, Victory Lane didn't yet exist), the first thing he asked for was a cold drink of buttermilk.

In 1936, Meyer became the first three-time winner of the Indianapolis 500, and a photograph was snapped of him enjoying his beverage of choice. An executive at the Milk Foundation (now the American Dairy Association) saw the photo and realized the potential publicity bonanza.

From that year on, the winner of the Indy 500 was supplied with a bottle of milk, although a couple of drivers have turned down the drink (Al Unser, Jr., most recently). To help seal the deal, today the

American Dairy Association of Indiana supplies the winner of the race with a cash award of $5,000 and a $500 check to the chief mechanic.

Chances are, the milk tradition would have continued even without the financial incentive provided by the ADA, for race-car drivers are notoriously ritualistic and superstitious, and probably would forsake the champagne of Super Bowl victors if drinking milk would allow them to emulate Meyer's success.

Are we overestimating the neurotic nature of race-car drivers? We think not, as our favorite Indy 500 superstition indicates. Ever since peanut shells were found on the seat of a crashed car in the 1940s, it has been considered bad luck to eat peanuts on the Speedway.

Submitted by Beth Fikar of West Chicago, Illinois. Thanks also to Anastasia L. Goodpasture of Greenfield, Indiana.

Does Cutting Paper With Sewing Scissors Really Ruin Them?

This Imponderable was submitted by one of our more prolific husband-and-wife pondering teams, Bill and Mary Ellen Jelen. They didn't indicate specifically that this is the case, but we have the sneaking suspicion that perhaps Bill has been invading the sewing kit to steal the scissors to cut out grocery coupons from the newspaper. Mary Ellen protests that using fabric scissors on paper will ruin them. Bill counters that the notion that sewing scissors will be ruined if used on paper is a pure myth. And now they come to us to solve their marital dispute. Can this marriage be saved?

We suspect that the marriage will survive this answer, but Bill, we're sorry to break it to you: Eat crow. Jeff Herman, executive director of the Society of American Silversmiths, told *Imponderables* that any cutting tool used on fabric must be razor-sharp. Paper is a harder material than fabric, and will eventually render sewing scissors duller and less efficient.

Furthermore, paper has clay content that comes off onto the scissor blades and dulls the cutting edge, according to J. F. Farrington, president of the National Association of Scissors and Shears Manufacturers. And Farrington adds:

> "While the dulling is slight and really can't be noticed if cutting only paper, it does over time cause problems with fabrics, particularly silk. Our suggestion is to keep your sewing scissors or shears separate."

Submitted by Bill and Mary Ellen Jelen of Akron, Ohio.

What Are the Black Specks in Some Vanilla Ice Creams? Do the Specks Affect the Taste? Why Do Some Brands Have Them and Others Not?

☞ Who would have thought that reader Frank D'Agostino could wring three questions about the black specks in vanilla ice cream? Let's take care of the first two right away, with the assistance of ice cream consultant Ed Marks:

> "The black specks are 'spent vanilla beans,' which have been ground. They are 'spent' because the vanilla flavor has already been extracted from them and they are, in effect, the residue of the vanilla beans."

If they don't add flavor, why put the specks into the ice cream in the first place? Samuel J. Nichols, marketing director of Quality Chekd Dairy Products Association, emphasizes the marketing considerations:

> "[The specks] designate that the product uses real vanilla as opposed to artificial vanilla flavoring. . . .

" 'Real' products generally have higher fat content, and thus higher prices, and consumers generally feel the product tastes better."

Lynn Anderson, of Borden's public affairs department, concurs, indicating that black specks indicate a "premium" product, and that an ice cream using beans would rightfully be considered to "most likely be a richer product, with an authentic taste."

As far as we can ascertain, Breyers was the first mass-marketed ice cream brand to contain vanilla specks. According to plant manager Tony Verlezza, Mr. Breyer himself started the practice in the early 1900s. Almost certainly, this is how speckled vanilla has become known as "Philadelphia ice cream" among folks in the dairy trade. Samuel Nichols notes that it wasn't until the 1970s that many other companies outside of the East Coast added specks.

And that might be for good reason, as Ed Marks elucidates:

"Until about thirty years ago, this ice cream was almost indigenous to the Philadelphia area. In fact, when served in other major metropolitan areas, customers would complain about the dirt in the ice cream."

Submitted by Frank D'Agostino of Hillside, New Jersey.

Why Is There No "U" After the "Q" in Qantas? How Did the Airline Get Its Strange Name?

Qantas is the oldest airline in the English-speaking world (only the Netherlands' KLM predates it). When Qantas was founded in 1921, the company's hard assets consisted of a one-room office, a wooden shed, and one biplane, shuttling farmers and graziers above the Australian Outback.

The original routes took passengers from Longreach, in the state of Queensland, to Brisbane (also in Queensland) and the city of Darwin, in the Northern Territory. The name of the company, Queensland and Northern Territory Aerial Services, Ltd., was appropriate indeed. Appropriate but cumbersome.

So an acronym was developed by taking the first letter of each word in the official name. Now Qantas is the official name of the company. And even though the corporation has moved its headquarters to Sydney and upgraded its routes to that of an international carrier, Qantas hasn't forgotten its roots:

"The original name has long since lost significance except as a reminder of brave and difficult origins, which may be why we feel such affection for it. That's why we are not being merely perverse when we pronounce it 'Kwontas' but spell it QANTAS."

Submitted by Paul Meehan of San Rafael, California.

Why Do Many Irish Names Have "O'" in Front of Them?

≈ We almost didn't research this Imponderable because we assumed that the "O'" was simply a variation of the abbreviation of "of" (as in "five o'clock" or "fillet o'fish"). Wouldn't it make sense that James O'Hara would be a descendant (i.e., "of") his father named O'Hara?

Close, but not quite. "O'" does mean "descendant" in dialect, but the Irish use it more specifically to mean "grandson of." This usage, according to Irish American Foundation's John Whooley, came into use after the time of St. Patrick (presumably, in the fifth or sixth century).

Of course, most Irish names are Anglicizations of Gaelic names. Shirley Starke, of the Mensa Irish special-interest group, told *Imponderables* that the original Gaelic "O" was not followed by an apostrophe but had an accent mark above it (Ó). Thus, O'Hara in Gaelic was expressed as "Ó Leadhra" (grandson of a man named Eadhra).

Why didn't they honor the father rather than the grandfather? Sometimes they did, for Mc (Irish) or Mac (Scottish) meant "son of."

Our guess is that more than a few readers might wonder how half the Irish population was described by "O," for daughters and granddaughters carried surnames that connote that they were of the opposite sex. We can only respond: Feminism wasn't an accident. As in most cultures, women were identified, essentially, as appendages of men.

Tom Horan, executive director of the American Irish Historical Association, told us that a few prefixes were developed especially for females. In Gaelic, "Ne" preceded surnames to indicate "daughter of" (e.g., Mary Ne Flannery) and "Béan" meant wife of (e.g., Béan O Reilly was the Gaelic equivalent of Mrs. O'Reilly). But these usages never made their way to the lands of English speakers, where, until recently, virtually all women adopted the names of their fathers or husbands for life.

Submitted by Pat Long of Oceanside, California.

How and Why Did Prisoners Get Into the License Plate Business? Is This Still a Common Practice?

⚘ Before the first license plate in the United States was issued in 1903, the city of Boston was clogged not only with automobiles, but with horses, pedestrians, and horse-drawn carriages. In order to rein in the chaos, Boston required driver's licenses and registrations starting in 1899.

At first, the license plates were manufactured by the Baltimore Enamel & Novelty Company (located in Baltimore, Maryland) and Ingram-Richardson Manufacturing Company of Beaver Falls, Pennsylvania. But according to license plate collector and historian Stewart Berg, a momentous shift occurred in 1920:

> "In 1920 the State Prison in Charlestown, Massachusetts, took over the manufacture of license plates. Plate #44 in 1920 was issued by the Registry of Motor Vehicles to Grover Cleveland's wife. The Massachusetts Correctional Institute at Cedar Junc-

tion today makes plates for Massachusetts and has made plates for other states, like New Hampshire and Maine."

How did correctional facilities "steal" this business away from private enterprise? For a historical overview, we contacted the Federal Bureau of Prisons. Archives specialist Anne Diestel responded:

"Historically, putting inmates to work has been considered an inmate management tool and a correctional technique. Work was a way of eliminating inmate idleness and could help a prisoner learn good work habits and acquire a skill that could be used once he was released from prison.

"The use of inmate labor has also been controversial throughout history. Private sector business and labor often argued that inmate-made products were unfair competition and were taking jobs away from law-abiding citizens. Because of this concern, prison systems have tried to have work available to inmates that would not cause undue competition with the private sector. In the 1920s and 1930s, the 'State-Use' system was developed, whereby inmate-made products were produced for the State's use and distribution. License plates are a good example of a 'State-Use' product."

In the 1920s, steel was a booming industry in the U.S., and many prisons took the opportunity to build smelting plants. As vehicle license plates were always issued by individual states, many other states besides Massachusetts decided to stamp plates out in their prisons. (Federal prisoners briefly produced plates for the federal government in the 1930s).

Today, at least 70 percent of all license plates are made in prison, according to Linda Rozell of the New York Department of Motor Vehicles. License plates are constantly going through technological improvements, which is making it more difficult to produce them solely in prisons. For example, New York has switched from galvanized steel to aluminum. And though they are still embossed in prison, the plates are sent out to private companies in order to have reflective sheeting put over them.

Although the prison population is growing by leaps and bounds, the potential of the license plate business isn't overwhelming. Despite the increasing number of new vehicles on the road, many states that used to issue new plates every year, or every fourth year, no longer demand plate changes at all—as yet, prisoners have not gotten into the "renewal sticker" business.

The Federal Prison System's UNICOR Corporation, established in 1934, may not make license plates, but it is a huge conglomerate, involved in more than 250 different industries (this diversification allows them to avoid conflicts with any particular private-sector industry). Unicor is allowed to sell only to federal government agencies, for they do have some advantages: inmate pay ranges from 23 cents to $1.15 per hour (with child-support, restitution, and other court-mandated fines docked from the inmate's wages).

UNICOR trains prisoners in everything from furniture-making to optics, and unlike most other government programs we can think of, actually runs at a profit. We can't help but think that the approximately 25 percent of Federal prisoners who participate in some aspect of the Federal Prison Industries program will be better trained than some of their state prison compatriots when they are released—there isn't much demand for skilled license plate manufacturers in private industry.

Submitted by Tim Poirier of Silver Spring, Maryland. Thanks also to Betsey Hemphill Pollikof of Towson, Maryland.

Why Don't You Ever See Zebras Being Ridden?

☙ We were so delighted to receive a question about zebras other than "Are zebras white with black stripes or black with white stripes?" (white with black stripes, honest!) that we sprang to action and contacted some of our favorite equine sources about this intriguing Imponderable. Some experts referred us to written sources, and we immediately saw two different approaches to explaining why none of us are likely to go zebraback riding in the near future.

Everyone is quick to indicate that the zebra's attitude toward humans is not one of great affection. From a personality point of view, perhaps the zebra deserves to be thought of more as an ass than a horse, if you know what we mean. The debate is a chicken-and-egg one: Is the zebra ornery by nature or has its behavior been biased by how we have treated them in the past?

Perhaps the strongest proponent of the "nature" argument is Wayne O. Kester, major domo of Equine Veterinary Consultant Services in Golden, Colorado:

> "We do not see zebras under saddle or in harness because their inherent disposition is such that they are not amenable to restraint or training by man. When it comes to handling them (as one would a horse), they are described as obstreperous, incorrigible, unpredictable and dangerous, because they will kick and bite defensively if restrained or in close quarters. They are regarded as untrainable. There are a few, very few exceptions, and even these are erratic and undependable.
>
> "On the other hand, zebras are not stupid. They are in fact very smart at self-preservation and protecting their own kind, which may be why man can't handle them."

The most common explanation by opponents of this argument is a practical one. Susan Lumpkin, director of communications at the National Zoological Park, cites Dorcas MacClintock's chapter "Efforts to Breed and Train Zebras" in *A Natural History of Zebras:*

> "She outlines instances of zebras being used in east and south Africa as pack animals and riding animals, so it has been done. She also offers the conventional explanation that zebras were not domesticated because they do not have the endurance that horses have evolved under many centuries of artificial selection, and because we already have horses, there's no point in reinventing them with zebras."

Furthering the "nurture" argument, Ed Hansen, executive director of the American Association of Zoo Keepers, points out that zebras who have been bottle-fed and reared by humans have been capable of being saddled and ridden: An occasional circus or petting zoo features these domesticated zebras. If they become conditioned to saddles, argues Hansen, they will likely accept a rider as well. Hansen concludes:

> "I would suspect that zebras have not been domesticated simply because of the abundance of horses, mules and oxen, not because of their 'wild' nature."

Submitted by Barry Kaminsky of Brooklyn, New York.

Why Don't the Seat Belts on Airline Passenger Seats Come Equipped With Shoulder Straps?

The Federal Aviation Agency doesn't require shoulder harnesses for passengers, and as far as we can tell, neither does any nation's regulators. And airlines are unlikely to volunteer to install them.

Why not?

1. Cost. As one pilot told *Imponderables,* the problem is "weight, weight, and weight." One study found that if every scheduled airline in the U.S. carried 1,000 more pounds per trip, it would cost millions of extra dollars per year.

Then there is the initial investment required to buy the apparatus. For jumbo jets, multiply the cost per 400 for each plane. Seat belts, and especially shoulder harnesses, are not inexpensive.

They must also be maintained amid the continual abuse by passengers; consider the problems with retraction that shoulder harnesses in automobiles present. While every airplane carries spare seat belts, spare shoulder straps would not be as easy to replace or fix on short notice.

2. Logistics. The problems involved in attaching a shoulder harness to any but window seats are considerable. In an automobile, the safety belt must be attached both to the wall and the floor—to what would the shoulder straps on aisle seats be attached?

3. Negligible Safety Benefits. United Airlines captain Michael Lauria points out that shoulder straps are most helpful during sudden stops, rare occurrences on jets, especially while aloft. And unlike in automobiles, airplane passengers don't face the risk of flying into a glass windshield. The emergency procedure stated by flight attendants in case of a crash (seat belt on, passenger bent over at waist bracing their hands against the seatback in front of them) also alleviates some of the devastating potential of flying forward in the seat.

Several pilots pointed out that a better course might be to install passenger seats "backward," virtually obviating any need for shoulder restraints. But that is unlikely to happen. According to Steven Price, many passengers object to facing the back of the plane, either because it induces airsickness or causes psychological disorientation.

Submitted by Kevin Bolduan of Portland, Oregon.

What Does the IRS Do With All the Tax Forms That Are Filed Every Year? How Long Does the IRS Keep Them?

☙ If your tax form happens to be of historic significance (let's say, for example, that you happen to be Al Capone), your form will likely be sent to the National Archives. But for those of us unlikely to be featured in *The Untouchables,* our processed tax forms are sent by an IRS service center to one of many Federal Records Centers throughout the United States.

Although taxpayers increasingly are filing electronically, the amount of paperwork generated by tax forms is not inconsiderable. So the method of disposal of these forms is specified in the *Internal Revenue Manual.* The 1040 form that you filed in, say, April 1995 usually will be sent to a Federal Records Center sometime between January 2 through March 31 of 1996, and kept for safekeeping until they are destroyed "on or after January 16, 6 years and 9 months after April 15 of the processing year."

Lest any tax dodgers think they are home free after this period, Ruth Hill, the otherwise amiable chief of campaign development for the IRS, issues a warning:

"Our Criminal Investigation Division may request longer retention for cases they are working [on], and returns on which a penalty of 50 percent or more has been assessed may also be retained longer.

"Of course, we maintain electronic records of all accounts indefinitely on our Information Document Retrieval System (IDRS)."

Take that, Al Capone.

Of course, every year the Federal Records Center faces the issue of how to dispose of the voluminous piles of old tax forms. How fitting that these documents to our pecuniary torture are sold as waste.

Lest you worry that your gross income will be read by an unsuspecting reveler at a ticker-tape parade, be assured that the IRS can sell paper records only after the documents have been destroyed "beyond legibility or reconstruction." Fiscally frugal to the end, the IRS even salvages the silver in film records.

It is this kind of fiscal responsibility that contributes to the marvelous efficiency of this vital American agency, an unfairly maligned institution that promotes fairness to all, collects revenues to make our country financially strong, and most important, continues not to audit us.

Submitted by Bruce Nordstrom of Maineville, Ohio.

What Does the "Old No. 7" on the Jack Daniel's Bottle Mean? Were There "Old Numbers 1 Through 6"?

Our guess is that there *were* numbers 1 through 6, but that is of little help in our quest to vanquish this enigma, for we couldn't get a definitive answer to what "Old No. 7" means. If it is of any comfort to reader Mike Teige, who submitted this Imponderable, please know that this question is of great interest to employees of the distillery itself. Since "Old Mr. Jack" was never kind enough to reveal the solution to this enduring mystery, we are left with the three most popular conjectures of Jack Daniel's workers:

The first, most obvious, and most likely theory is that Jack didn't get his whiskey down right the first few tries. Not until he got to his seventh batch, perhaps, did Jack know he made a whiskey fit for the ages.

Second, and more intriguing perhaps, our Jack had an active romantic streak. Could Jack have been playing seven women off against each other simultaneously? Could Jack have been paying a tribute to his seventh conquest? (Even if the "lucky" woman could get over being his seventh trophy, would she have been thrilled to be called "old" as well?)

Third, and most implausible, Jack evidently had a friend who had opened and closed a string of six unsuccessful businesses. Could Jack have conjured up good luck by harnessing the lucky powers of the number seven? Evidently, the seventh business, a hardware store, did indeed succeed.

Submitted by Mike Teige of Seattle, Washington.

Why Doesn't Aluminum Foil Feel Hot When It Comes Out of a Roaring Oven?

❧ Rest assured, "if you stuck your finger into a hot oven, the aluminum would be hot," writes James Plumb, director of communications for the Aluminum Association. Let's say you put into your 400° Fahrenheit oven a baked potato wrapped in aluminum foil, along with a meat loaf in a ceramic container covered by a glass top. All of the foods and containers will eventually attain the temperature designated on the thermostat, but at varying speeds.

Different metals have varying abilities to spread heat quickly and evenly—those that are best at this task are referred to as having a "high conduction rate." One of the reasons why aluminum is used for foil is that it is, as a representative of Alumax Foils put it, "an excellent conductor of heat." Only three other metals have a higher conduction rate: gold, silver, and copper—all much more expensive commodities.

But why does the aluminum foil cool off so much faster than, say, the ceramic casserole dish or the glass top? Once the foil is removed, it is as responsive to the cooler ambient air as it was to the hot air inside of the oven. Aluminum quickly releases its heat into the cooler room.

But one crucial difference between aluminum foil and the glass top or the casserole dish is its thinness, as Jeff Glenning, a materials engineer at Reynolds Metals Company, explains:

> "Since the foil is very thin, the heat does not have to travel far in the metal before it is released into the air. If you think about it, aluminum foil is the only metal that is used in cooking that is this thin. Reynolds Wrap . . . is less than a thousandth of an inch thick. Pots and pans are usually made out of much thicker metal, sometimes aluminum. But since they are much thicker than foil, these metallic objects trap heat inside the metal for a longer period of time. Thus, the high heat conduction rate and the shape of the foil allow it to cool before you touch it, giving the illusion that it was never hot."

Glenning adds that another physical characteristic of aluminum adds to the "not hot misconception." While aluminum has high conductivity, it has low *emissivity* (heat radiated from the aluminum's surface). Put your hand an inch above boiling water and the heat will be oppressive; put your hand an inch above a hotter piece of aluminum and you will not feel intense heat. Glenning says that "the aluminum would not feel hot until the skin actually comes in contact with the surface of the aluminum (conduction)."

Submitted by Marc Brewer of Reston, Virginia. Thanks also to Debbie Marcus of Parma, Ohio.

David Feldman

Why Do Tuba Bells Face Up Rather Than Toward the Audience?

❧ Paul Droste, the director of the Brass Band of Columbus, and former president of the North American Brass Band Association, told *Imponderables* that although a major factor in the positioning of the tuba bell is simply tradition, there are acoustic considerations as well. The sound of a tuba tends to be outsized, just like the girth of the instrument itself. According to Droste,

> "A bell-front tuba may be too direct, producing too much volume, plus other extraneous noises. The bell-up instruments blend better, especially in good indoor concert halls."

When high volume is desirable, such as in military and marching bands and outdoor concerts, tubas and sousaphones are usually placed bell-front. Professor of Music David Henning, who is director of the University of Iowa Marching Band, says that the bell-forward position produces a slightly cleaner sound, with more "presence."

When you think about it, all brass instruments feature directional sound. It doesn't matter much whether a listener sits in front of or behind a drummer or violinist. But someone sitting directly in front of a tuba with a bell-front will experience a skewed version of reality—a little like hearing Mozart for the first time by enduring the bass thump of the stereo speakers of your upstairs neighbor.

Submitted by Brian Uri of Alexandria, Virginia.

Why Does "Smoke" Escape From the Bottle Just After Soda Is Opened?

Who would better know the answer to this Imponderable than a senior consumer affairs specialist at Coca-Cola, Lori A. McManes?

> "The 'smoke' seen escaping from a bottle of soft drink just after it is opened is condensed water vapor. Water vapor is present along with carbon dioxide in the bottle's head space, the space between the liquid soft drink and the bottle cap. When the bottle is opened, pressure inside the bottle is quickly released and these gases escape.
>
> "This sudden release of pressure causes a rapid reduction in temperature in the area surrounding the opened bottle. This decrease in temperature, in turn, causes the water vapor that has escaped to condense, and gives it the wispy appearance of 'smoke.' "

An old friend of *Imponderables,* Pepsi's Christine Jones, says that we see the same effect all the time in our everyday lives when we walk outside on a cold day and see our breaths creating "smoke."

Submitted by Suzanne Saldi of West Berlin, New Jersey.

Toby and Keesha have successfully exploded a toilet in the first floor girls' room...

HURRY!!

I THINK WE NEED A DOZEN MORE TOWEL MACHINES!

$\mathcal{W}hat$ Is the Meaning of the "Emergency Feed" Notation Found on Most Paper Towel Dispensers?

✢ What kind of emergency could possibly involve a paper towel? Half the time, dispensers seem to be out of towels, and we hardly consider *that* a crisis.

You won't find "Emergency Feed" signs on the lowest-tech dispensers, the "self-feeding" variety that require you to pull out the towels one at a time. We have no idea why anyone felt the need to improve upon this kind of dispenser; one can see readily if a towel is available and can reach up and take as many as needed.

Ah, but progress cannot be stopped, so the "roll-towel dispenser" was born, a high-tech paper version of what used to be a cotton (and usually dirty) towel on a roll. E. T. Bond, sales director of paper giant Kimberly-Clark, explains why roll-towel dispensers feature the "Emergency Feed" notation:

> "These dispensers often have a timing device that will control the length of towel and how often the towel dispenses. You've probably stood in a rest room with wet hands, grabbed the

towel, pulled it down, and then, as you're drying your hands, heard a clanging sound as the timer pushes another towel into view after a delay of five to ten seconds.

"Often these roll-towel dispensers, even though they are large, formidable plastic objects, do not perform as designed and *no* towel is visible. That's why even though the dispensing action is supposed to be automatic, an emergency feed feature is always included (usually at the right-hand side of the dispenser, since most people are right-handed).

"The emergency feed feature enables the hapless, dripping-hands user to manually start ('feed') enough of the towel through the front of the dispenser to grab hold and pull off the appropriate amount."

We're still not sure that the inability to grab a paper towel constitutes an emergency, but we appreciate the attempt to help us dry our hands. We would just as soon have warning signs displayed on the automatic hand dryers, now often found in lieu of paper towels: "Warning: Regardless of long you stand in front of this machine, and regardless of how vigorously you rub your extremities together, you will never, ever, ever, leave this rest room with dry hands."

Submitted by Marian Ruggles Wenck and William Wenck, Jr. of Old Lyme, Connecticut.

Why Do Heinz Ketchup Bottles in Restaurants Have "Restaurant Package—Not for Resale" on the Label?

Literally the only difference between the 14-ounce bottle of Heinz ketchup that you find in a restaurant and the one you buy in a store is the neck label referred to in the question. The ketchup is exactly the same. The bottle is exactly the same.

So why the need for the different labels? Heinz separates its retail (grocery store) and foodservice (restaurants, hotels, and other institutions) divisions. The sales and distribution networks are completely different. Beth Adams, of Heinz U.S.A., told *Imponderables* that internally, the neck labels are used to designate inventory if the destination of certain boxes is in doubt.

We've always assumed that the "Not for Resale" warning indicated that there was a black market in restaurant ketchup, but Deb Magness, manager of communications at Heinz U.S.A., demurs. The price differential between wholesale grocery and restaurant accounts isn't large enough to motivate such clandestine behavior. Magness claims that restaurants, who pay a slight premium to display the best-selling ketchup, prefer a product created specifically for them. As she puts it, "The tabletop is important real estate to us." Indeed, Heinz and Sweet and Low are the two most commonly found brand names on restaurant tables. It behooves Heinz to keep its foodservice customers satisfied; if a distinctive label helps, Heinz is happy to oblige.

While we were still unsure if we had gotten to the bottom of this Imponderable, Deb distracted us with a bit of advice that we wanted to share with you about the crucial problem of how to get Heinz ketchup out of a new bottle. Heinz discourages insertions of knives into the bottle. Likewise, pounding on the bottom of the bottle is out (it actually helps perpetuate the vacuum seal). The best method, according to Magness, is to tilt the ketchup bottle at an angle (not straight down), and jab the bottle where the "57's" are molded into the glass. The 57's are located right where the ketchup forms a natural seal. If you tap the 57's properly, you will break the seal and the ketchup, thick as it is, will pour quickly. Well, quicker than molasses, anyway.

Submitted by Herbert Kraut of Forest Hills, New York. Thanks also to Jeffrey Chavez of El Segundo, California; Jerry A. Buegler of Minneapolis, Minnesota; J. A. Wethmeller of Sun City West, Arizona; Eugene Fales of Mukilteo, Washington; Roy Preece of Massillon, Ohio; and Mark A. Silverman of Daly City, California.

SPECIAL THANKS to the late Beth Adams, a valued source at Heinz U.S.A.

Why Are Funeral Homes So Large? How Do They Utilize All That Space?

❧ Compared to most other businesses, the funeral trade is both more and less predictable. The good news? If you are the only funeral home in a town, you are virtually guaranteed to win the business of every citizen—exactly once. So the funeral home business is remarkably recession-resistant; potential clients do not have the luxury of deferring the purchase of funeral services.

The bad news? On a day-to-day basis, though, the flow of business is highly erratic. When considering the size of a funeral home, the owner must assume that if the home averages 365 services a year, the client base will not be considerate enough to die once every twenty-four hours. John Rodenburg, vice president of Federated Funeral Directors of America, puts it more delicately:

> "On the first floor, there are usually at least two viewing rooms or chapels. Wanting to deal sensitively with the bereaved, no funeral director would want to turn away a family because he was 'full.' Nor would he want to say, 'We're busy today, please

come back tomorrow.' Thus you have two, three, or more visitation areas, even though only one might be in use when you visit a funeral home."

Many funeral homes are converted residences. Rodenburg points out that as the upper class fled downtown areas for the suburbs, many funeral directors bought large, two-story residences:

"In order to provide full service (after all, someone could die at any hour of the day or night), the proprietor lived in the funeral home. He and his family lived on the second floor and the funeral home was on the first floor. Most funeral homes still have someone living in them."

A leading consultant in the funeral industry, Harold C. Raether, warns that there is a tendency in too many funeral directors to "build a memorial to themselves." In many small towns, in particular, funeral homes have a tendency of dwarfing the neighboring buildings and appearing out of scale.

Even if the funeral director's family does not live in the home, space is still at a premium. Consider all of the functional rooms that a full-service funeral home contains:

• The chapels (usually at least two) are commonly the largest rooms in the home. They must be large enough to contain not only the loved ones of the deceased, but also the casket, the flowers, and a pulpit for the clergy and speakers. Many chapels contain adjoining "family rooms," where the family of the deceased is afforded some privacy but is still provided a direct view of the deceased, flowers, and clergy.

• State rooms or visitation rooms—where wakes or visitation can be made without formal services.

• Family lounge—usually found adjacent to the carport, this is where the bereaved can rest before services, before or after private viewings, etc.

• Coffee or smoking lounges—Funeral directors don't particularly want bereaved parties to wander around the facilities. If the staff is busy, say, attending to the casket selection of one family, a space needs to be provided for another family to wait in a pleasant atmosphere.

- Public rest rooms.
- Casket selection—Even small funeral homes usually have between twelve and twenty-eight caskets on display. Obviously, this requires a large room, one not in the middle of client flow, so it is often placed in the basement. Some funeral homes also contain separate clothing and vault displays, as well.
- Arrangements room—where the funeral director meets with families to "close the deal."
- Mausoleum entombment, marker displays, and flower shops —these can be found in some large funeral homes.

All of the above are rooms that most families will see when dealing with a funeral home. But then there are the rooms that the funeral homes don't want you to see, because they are where unpleasant tasks are performed:

Forwarding/Receiving Area—where corpses are brought into and out of the home.

Crematorium.

Preparation room—where the body is embalmed and prepared for viewing.

Dressing room—where the final details are made for viewing. This is necessary if the funeral home, for example, doesn't want outside hairdressers or cosmeticians working in the same room while they are "preparing" another body.

And then there are the mundane areas delegated to employees: funeral home offices; storage areas (all those chairs in the chapel or state rooms have to go somewhere); clergy room (in many homes, clergy are provided a place to prepare for the service and given a separate entrance to the chapel); music room (often above and in back of the chapel, with visual access to the pulpit, it must contain tape-recording equipment, but often holds an organ); dormitories (a place for nonfamily employees to sleep).

Given all the requirements inside the funeral home, the proprietor is stuck with another financial headache: The rule of thumb is that for every square foot inside the funeral home, four times as much footage should be devoted to the land outside of the home. Ample parking must be provided not only for the grieving, but for the unusually large investment that funeral directors must make in its own vehicles. According to Rodenburg, most funeral homes have three to six garages. Often, these garages are attached to the main structure, adding to the home's bulk.

Rodenburg adds that most modern funeral homes are designed on one level to provide easier access for the disabled, making new homes even more sprawling affairs. So maybe we should be asking why funeral homes aren't larger.

Submitted by Stephen Maxon of Adams Center, New York; Matthew Lawrence of Watertown, New York; and Thomas Nathon of Watertown, New York.

What Good Do the Height Clearance Signs on Highway Overpasses Do When Truckers Can't See Them Far Enough in Advance to React?

Although this Imponderable came from a reader, we've often pondered this ourselves. If, say, a tunnel is too low for a tall truck, isn't that sign in front of the tunnel warning about the low clearance just a teensy bit too late?

We heard from four different traffic safety experts, and the consensus answer to what good these signs are was: not very much good at all. Typical was the droll response of Robert W. O'Brien, director of public relations for the National Safety Council:

> "A clearance sign probably means little to a trucker who is about to drive under an overpass at 65 mph. Of course, if the top of his 13′8″ trailer were to be peeled back by a 13′6″ overpass—during a crunchingly noisy and abrupt stop—he would at least be able to tell his dispatcher exactly how he wrecked the rig."

Although the standards for maximum dimensions for vehicles varies from state to state, 13 feet, 6 inches in height is the limit in most states. Most overhead structures on roadways have a clearance of at least 14 feet, with 16-feet clearances on interstate highways. If a truck exceeds the maximum height, a permit must be granted by the state in order for it to be driven. David Hensing, deputy executive director of the American Association of State Highway and Transportation Officials, told *Imponderables* that along with the permit is

"a designated route, which may require indirect or circuitous travel, but which is selected to avoid conflicting overhead structures."

But not all overhead structures meet even the 13 feet, 6 inches standard, so Hensing reports that the *Manual on Uniform Traffic Control Devices* calls for

". . . placement of Low Clearance signs on or immediately in advance of structures where 'clearances are less than the maximum vehicle height plus 12 inches.'

"These signs show the actual clearance to the nearest inch. In addition, provisions of this Section call for placement of a sign indicating a clearance restriction ahead at 'the nearest intersecting road or wide point in the road at which a vehicle can detour or turn around.' "

Hensing claims that even the smallest lettering required for the diamond-shaped "warning sign could be seen by a driver with 20/30 vision from 500 feet away,

". . . more than adequate to bring an over-height vehicle to a halt, assuming its driver failed to see the height limitation warning at the preceding intersection or wide point.

"Actually, sign visibility is more frequently affected negatively by restrictions such as utility poles, other structures, and sight restrictions imposed by vertical roadway geometry such as a 'dip' in the roadway. However, without researching the issue, I do not believe that the striking of substandard height overhead structures by vehicles not exceeding legal height maximums is a very frequent accident type in the United States."

While conceding that overhead signs do "very little good, I am afraid," Jan Balkin, of the American Trucking Association, indicates that most truckers never face this emergency:

> "Some of the specialized atlases available to truckers have low underpass locations, and dispatchers may give the drivers this type of information, but on unfamiliar routes on the less-traveled highways, that information may not be available. Signs attached to overpasses can be seen, but at highway speeds, truckers may not have the time necessary to react. When that is the case, the truck gets stuck."

Ironically, the oversized trucks with special permits for height are less likely to "get stuck" than twelve-footers. Not only must they conform to an established route, but drivers are constantly on the lookout for unfamiliar structures that may entrap them.

Glen A. Carriker, of the Missouri Safety Center, reports that ever since uniform clearance signs have been posted, highway engineers have done a better job of posting warning signs far in advance, so that truckers need not rely solely on the too-late overhead signs.

Submitted by Jason Ball of Waco, Texas.

$\mathcal{W}hy$ Are Insects Attracted to Ultraviolet and Repelled by Yellow?

☞ Insects aren't vain. Don't assume that a mosquito will shun a yellow light because it casts an unflattering sheen on its brownish wings.

But insects are sensitive beings, or more properly, *visually* sensitive, as Steven J. Schutz, of the University of California's Mosquito Control Research Library, explains:

"Many insects are most sensitive to the ultraviolet and green wavelengths. Since ultraviolet wavelengths tend to predominate in the sky and green wavelengths predominate in vegetation, this combination may enhance detection of objects an insect is likely to encounter during flight.

"It is not true that insects are repelled by yellow. Some may be less attracted to yellow because they are less sensitive to the yellow wavelengths; others may actually be attracted by yellow. For example, yellow plastic panels coated with sticky material are commonly used to control whiteflies and other pests in greenhouses; the whiteflies are attracted to and stick to the panels. Many flower-visiting insects, including honeybees, exhibit preferences for yellow and blue flowers. Red light *does* tend to be less attractive, since most insects have poor reception of red wavelengths."

So even though a white porch light might attract more moths than a yellow light, it isn't because the bugs don't "like" yellow; more likely, they weren't attracted to the light in the first place. An official from the National Pest Control Association told *Imponderables* that ultraviolet black lights have traditionally been the most popular components of "bug zappers," devices that lure insects inside only to "fry" them with an electrical grid. Schutz agrees that the UV light is most effective in enticing insects, but no single color by itself is sufficient to keep insects from their appointed task of making our lives a little more annoying.

Submitted by Douglas Watkins, Jr., of Hayward, California. Thanks also to Renee Gonsiewski of Villa Park, Illinois; and David Shelley of St. Paul, Minnesota.

I_S the Red Color in Cooked Beef Simply Blood? If So, Why Doesn't the Meat Discolor When Exposed to Oxygen?

❦ Many folks who don't like rare meat cite as the reason: "I can't stand the sight of blood." Actually, they can't stand the sight of myoglobin. For this water-soluble protein is most responsible for the red color we associate with meat.

For those of you who consider eating a rare steak the gastronomic equivalent of vampirism, you'd be surprised to learn what Dennis Buege, of the meat sciences department at the University of Wisconsin, told us: Less than 20 percent of the normal amount of blood found in living tissue remains in a piece of meat sold in a supermarket. Myoglobin functions much the same way as hemoglobin does in our bodies. Hemoglobin carries oxygen from our lungs to our bodies; myoglobin stores the oxygen the hemoglobin has brought to the tissues.

But myoglobin is also what's called a "protein pigment." It helps color the meat. When meat is fresh cut and not exposed to oxygen, it has a purplish color; once exposed to air (oxygenation), the muscle tissue quickly changes to red.

This red color is what we associate with raw beef at the meat counter. Although it might seem that the clear film wrapping used to cover meat in markets is designed to prevent oxygen from attacking the meat, Buege informed us that the opposite is the case. The film is designed to *permit* oxygen to pass through in order to maintain the red color that consumers prefer. Oxygenation also explains why the inside of a package of ground beef looks different in color than the bright red exterior—for only the inside of the meat has been "deprived" of oxygen and has retained its natural coloring.

Buege bemoans our aesthetic preference for "red meat," because it accelerates the spoilage rate. If fresh meat were vacuum-packed, and did not go through the oxygenation process, we might be deprived of the chance to choose between fire-engine-red meats

David Feldman

in refrigerated cases, but it would extend the shelf life of fresh meat from the current 2 to 4 days to an astonishing 10 to 14 days.

Why doesn't *cooked* meat discolor again when confronted with the ambient air? According to Janet Collins Williams, vice president of scientific and technical affairs for the American Meat Institute, the color change caused by oxygenation is reversible in the muscle

> "as long as there remains adequate stored energy in the muscle for the pigment conversion. However, once the energy is depleted, and/or once the protein portion of the pigment is heated (when the muscle is cooked), the color is 'set.' . . . Depending upon the degree of heating of the tissue (degree of doneness in the meat), the protein is actually denatured, and the original color(s) is destroyed. Therefore, the meat does not change color or discolor when exposed to air—it is stable."

Submitted by Doug Huxsol of Towanda, Kansas.

Why Are Dinner Plates Round?

✧ With the research help of Harry Frost, director of the Dyson-Perrins Museum in Worcester, England, Doris Nixon, director of educational services for the National Bridal Service, sent a fascinating letter tracing the history of plates. Here are some of the highlights:

> "It has been generally assumed that pottery was preceded by basket-making. Most baskets were round, for ease in weaving. Prehistoric man, or rather woman, strengthened basketwork bowls by smearing the outside with clay. The idea of pottery may have started when such a basket was accidentally burnt. Fired clay pieces with basketwork imprints dating from 15,000 to 10,000 B.C. have been found in Gambles Cave in Kenya.
>
> "The other most common freehand method of modeling pottery was coiling, the building up of vessels by long coils. With this method, forming round shapes is the most natural construction method.
>
> "Casting involving liquid clay was used in ancient Pales-

tine, but this method has only been used in Europe since A.D. 1730. To make a plate in a shape other than round involves casting, which is more expensive than other methods used.

"The introduction of the potter's wheel, probably man's oldest machine, marked the beginning of the mechanization of pottery. The earliest known use of the potter's wheel was in the Mesopotamian town of Worka, 5000 B.C. Potters also used wheels during the Indus Valley civilization, 3250–3000 B.C., as did the Mayan people for making ceramic toys for their children. By Old Testament times, 2000 B.C., the potter's wheel was in common use in Southern Palestine. In fact, one of the gates of Jerusalem was called the 'Gate of Potsherds' (broken pots).

"So, going back in history as far as 5000 B.C., plates were round, as they were made by the potter's wheel."

Some cultures also used wooden plates, and fashioned them from found trees. If trees were square, they probably would have fashioned square dinner plates.

Even today, round plates have distinct advantages for the manufacturers. According to Judy Stern of Noritake Co.,

"Other shapes can be made, but oval and square pieces, for example, must be cast in a mold. This process is much more expensive, more labor-intensive, and takes more time."

Round plates also tend to be more durable than other shapes. Helen Grayson, of the American Restaurant China Council, told *Imponderables* that rectangular plates, with sharp edges, are more likely to chip or break off.

In the 1930s and 1940s, square plates were in vogue briefly, but then went out of style. Ever since, other nonround shapes have been far more popular in Europe than in North America, but china manufacturers keep trying to spring other shapes on a public perfectly satisfied with round plates: fish plates in the shape of fish; oval plates for steaks; and octagonal plates for aesthetes.

But Americans seem to always come around to Ms. Nixon's

point of view: "If you can't improve history, don't attempt to change it! The fact of the matter is, round plates will continue to be."

Submitted by Laura Arvidson of Westville, Indiana.

SPECIAL THANKS to Betty Feagans of the Royal China and Porcelain Companies, for her help.

What Causes the "Pop-Pop" Noise of Helicopters?

☞ Much to our surprise, "pop" is the term actually used by pilots to describe the distinctive noises generated by helicopters. Entire books have been written about the racket initiated by choppers, but John Shaw, technical director of the American Helicopter Society, explains the common threads that all "pops" share:

> "The 'pop-pop' noise is created by the whirling rotor blades as they sweep through the air above the helicopter. It may be helpful to think of the air 'swept' by the rotor blades as forming a large, thin 'disk.' 'Pop-pop' sounds occur when some spot on this disk is 'ready' to create a sharp disturbance in the air (which we hear as noise, like a balloon popping in the distance) when a blade passes through that spot. The noise is a sequence of 'pops' because the individual blades pass one after the other, 'pop-pop-pop,' through the noise-generating spot."

The generic name for this type of noise is "blade slap," and three discrete types of blade slap have been identified:

1. Ernie Stephens, president of Werewolf Aviation ("Driving 'Egg Beaters' is what we do best!"), told us that as the rotor blades spin, each one leaves a wake of turbulent air behind it:

"The following blade then advances and 'slaps' into its wake, causing a 'pop' sound. This phenomenon is called *blade-wake interaction,* and is similar to the hull of a boat hitting a wave."

2. The second noise is duller than the first, perhaps more accurately described as "thud-thud" than "pop-pop." John Shaw describes it:

"Each rotor blade, as it moves along, pushes the air away in front of it. This causes pressure waves to radiate ahead. We hear the pressure waves as sound. The faster the blade moves through the air, the more intense the pressure waves become. The time of fastest motion is when the blade, once per revolution, reaches the area where it is sweeping 'forward' in the direction of flight. The blade passes through the 'spot' very quickly, so the most intense pressure waves occur in a burst. . . ."

3. In certain times, a helicopter can cause a mini–sonic boom, as Shaw explains:

"When the helicopter is flying *very* fast, the forward speed of the helicopter and the speed of a forward-sweeping blade combine to approach the speed of sound. The pressure waves ahead of the rapidly moving blade cannot move fast enough to get away from the blade. The waves build up and combine to form a shock wave—a small version of the shock wave ahead of a supersonic airplane. The airplane forms a shock wave constantly, but the helicopter forms its shock wave only briefly as each blade sweeps forward through the spot where its speed is nearly supersonic. As each shock wave forms and collapses, we hear a 'pop.' The resulting 'pop-pop-pop' noise is most noticeable when the helicopter is approaching the listener."

Ernie Stephens says that this phenomenon creates the most "pop-like" sound of the three, and was frequently heard in households during the Vietnam War via American HUH-1 Huey helicopters. According to Stephens,

> "The rotor blades on this particular aircraft turn so fast they compress the air while advancing through it. Newer helicopter rotor systems are more efficient and spin at speeds slow enough to eliminate most of this noise."

Submitted by J. D. McNair of Muncie, Indiana.

Why Do Mole Hairs Tend to Grow Faster and Appear Darker Than Other Body Hairs?

❧ Moles are benign tumors of the skin and may contain hairs or remain hairless. Moles form deep down in the skin, in cells full of pigment, at the same level where hair follicles are formed, as dermatologist Gerald C. Gladstone explains:

> "Hairs grow from a structure called the hair follicle, which is an extension downward of the epidermis into the second layer of the skin, the dermis. The hair follicles that grow in association with moles are bigger and deeper than hair follicles in many other locations, and certainly on the surrounding, relatively hairless areas of skin where moles often occur."

The same melanin pigment that makes moles darker than surrounding epidermis is responsible for many mole hairs being darker than nearby hair. As Pepper Pike, Ohio, dermatologist Jerome Litt puts it:

"The color of hair depends upon the amount of melanin. If the moles are dark, the same pigment cells that are in the mole are in the hair. The mole hair will have the same pigment as the skin underneath."

Furthermore, the fact that mole hairs tend to be coarser and thicker than surrounding body hairs tends to make mole hairs *appear* to be darker than they are.

And why do mole hairs grow faster than surrounding hairs? The consensus of the seven dermatologists we contacted is that the premise is incorrect. Dermatologist Samuel Selden states the case emphatically:

"Mole hair does not grow faster or more easily than the surrounding hair. Because the hair roots may be positioned closer to the surface in the elevated moles, it may appear that these hairs will appear quicker after plucking. But hair grows at a consistent rate for the entire cutaneous surface and I have read nothing to suggest there is an exception to this constant growth rate in moles."

Dr. Joseph Bark concurs with Selden, and dares us to take the "mole hair challenge":

"Mole hair grows at the same rate as other hair in the vicinity, a fact you can prove to yourself by plucking the hair out of a mole you can watch and the hairs adjacent to it, and watching them all grow back at the same rate. The reason we *think* this is that the hairs are usually genetically coarser than the other hairs in the area, and so are more noticeable."

If any *Imponderables* readers want to throw down the gauntlet and take the mole hair challenge, feel free to report your findings; we'll be glad to share them.

On a related note, Dr. Gladstone wanted us to dispel a myth that he encounters often in his practice, and one that has been posed to us as an Imponderable more than once. Again, it is an in-

David Feldman

dication of how optical illusions have created the misconceptions we've punctured above:

> "There is a common myth that shaving makes hairs grow faster. Actually, there is no conceivable reason this should occur, but it seems to be the case simply because when a hair is shaved off, it has no perceptible length above the surface of the skin.
>
> "Within twenty-four hours, there is a projection of the hair that can be easily seen and felt, and the difference between the smooth skin of one day and the stubble of the next is so dramatic that it seems as if the hair is growing quickly. When a hair is much longer, that same one-third of a millimeter that it grows in twenty-four hours does not seem to contribute a whole lot to its length, giving the impression that it may not have grown very much at all."

Two of the dermatologists asked us to lance another myth about moles. Because moles, rarely, can turn cancerous, some patients are afraid to pluck hairs for fear of "stirring up" the mole. As Dr. Bark states:

> "Does it damage a mole to pluck it? Will it cause cancer? No, in both cases. Any cancers that arise in a mole would have arisen anyway, regardless of plucking hairs from them."

Submitted by Ryan Bouts of Glencoe, Minnesota. Thanks also to Louis Dottoli, Jr., of Erial, New Jersey.

Why Do Elevator Doors Open and Close Before Changing Directions?

This phenomenon can be observed most often when an elevator arrives with a sole passenger before you have had a chance to punch a call button. The passenger leaves the elevator. The hallway indicator lights show that the elevator is headed up. But you want to go down. You enter the elevator anyway and push "L" for lobby. Usually, the elevator will go up anyway. But occasionally, you will luck out and the elevator will change its mind and head south, most often because another elevator has been given the honor of picking up the person who called the elevator at a higher floor. But before the elevator goes down, the doors open again, the doors reclose, the "up" arrow inside the elevator turns to "down," and the elevator heads to the lobby.

Why is the extra step necessary? We got the answer from the biggest name in the industry, the Otis Elevator Company. Chris Cowles, of the communication department, consulted with John Kendall, director of advanced research, and Bruce Powell, principal engineer and dispatching expert. They agreed that there is no technical reason for this policy.

Sensibly enough, safety requirements demand that elevators not leave a floor without the doors being closed. But the opening and closing of doors is a simple signal to passengers that the car is changing directions, especially for those who have just entered the car. Of course, the hallway lights indicate the directional change, as well. But a light in the hallway is of scant help to those inside the elevators, who without the little door shuffle would be hostages in an elevator car going the "wrong way on a one-way street."

Submitted by Charles Myers of Ronkonkoma, New York.

What Are the Peephole-Like Circular Holes Found Toward the Top of Elevator Doors?

To allay any fears you might have, those *aren't* peepholes. At least that's what the experts at Otis say. We thought they may be vent holes, for many of us exhibit a persistent desire to breathe, but that's not what those holes are for either. Chris Cowles writes:

"These openings are for insertion of a special device called a 'drop-key' that allows the hall-side doors to be unlocked. Unbeknownst to many, there are two sets of doors on an elevator—elevator doors and hallway doors. In the event of a malfunction where the doors do not open, rescuers can gain entry to the car from the hallway by using a drop-key."

Submitted by Catherine Greene of Silver Spring, Maryland. Thanks also to Jeff Mihalich of Dorsey, Illinois.

Why Does the University of Miami Put a Big "U" on Its Football Helmets Instead of "M" or "UM"? Does the "U" Stand for University? And Why Did They Choose a Nickname With Such a Negative Image as "The Hurricanes"?

❧ The saga of the University of Miami "U" begins with the dissatisfaction of the Athletic Federation, the fund-raising branch of the athletic department, about the many changes over the years in the Hurricanes' uniforms. The Federation was determined to achieve a distinctive logo that could be used for all of its competitive sports.

The federation hired a local designer, Bill Bodenheimer, to create a logo, and his conclusion was novel. Too many major universities, including several sports powerhouses, happened to have initials of UM. Think of all the big state universities that start with "M" (Michigan, Maryland, Minnesota, Missouri, Montana, and Maine—come to think of it, not all UM schools are sports powerhouses!) and you'll realize the canniness of Bodenheimer's idea. Any university *could have* appropriated the "U," but none had done so. Only one state's name (Utah) begins with a "U," and none of the one hundred biggest cities in the U.S. begins with a "U." Therefore, of the major universities, UM has a virtual monopoly on the letter "U."

Furthermore, Bodenheimer liked the "U" because of its graphic possibilities. According to the school's public relations department:

"[the "U"] lent itself to inserting silhouetted athletes in the middle of the 'U' to establish distinctive logos for each sport as well as slogans like 'U gotta believe' and 'U is great.' "

Presumably, the English department did not sign off on that last slogan.

While we had the University of Miami's ears, we thought we'd ask how the school came up with the "Hurricanes" nickname. To us, that's not the most brilliant P.R.—it's a little like calling the UCLA team "The Smogs," Northwestern's team the "Wind Chills," or Columbia University's team "The Muggers."

Alas, the origins of the nickname are obscure. One theory is that the 1927 football team came up with the name after the catastrophic hurricane of 1926; others speculate that the 1926 team chose the name after their opening game was postponed because of a hurricane.

The *1994 University of Miami Football Media Guide* acknowledges the dubious imagery of the nickname but provides a winning riposte:

"But as one UM official rationalized in the 60's, 'Does anyone think Chicago is overrun by bears just because the town has a football team by that name?' "

Submitted by Daniel Phelka of Troy, Michigan.

Why Are Giant Pandas, at Least in Zoos, Given Double Names Such as "Ling-Ling" and "Hsing-Hsing"?

Doubling of a name is common in Chinese culture, and not just for pandas. As Bob Hansen, president of the American Association of Zoo Keepers, puts it, "Repetitive names in Chinese are a form of endearment associated with children."

Dr. Gang Xu of Jefferson University provides an example:

"The Chinese custom and term of endearment is to take one-syllable names and double them. For example, my son is named Ke Xu. His nickname is Koko, which is a doubling of the first name. This kind of nickname is used by family and close friends."

Those less close to his son would call him "Xu Ke." So doubling the name of a panda is a type of diminutive, the equivalent of calling Mike "Mikey," or Sandra "Sandy," and is an indication of how treasured and beloved pandas are in Chinese culture.

A San Diego Zoo animal curator of Chinese descent, who prefers for us not to use any of *her* names, told *Imponderables* that the Chinese often give pandas double names simply to make them easier for foreigners to remember and pronounce. By contrast, elephants and lions are often assigned numbers (for record-keeping purposes) rather than names.

Not all pandas are given double names—Su Lin and Yuan Jing are two such examples. But the majority of the most famous pandas have doubled names, and the designations can be inspired by a quality, a physical object, or even its place of birth. Perhaps the most famous panda ever in North America was Ling-Ling (which literally means "slim and agile"), but according to Susan Lumpkin, director of communications of the Friends of the National Zoo, this name

"is a general term of affection applied to young Chinese girls, and refers to the tinkling sound created by the bells they sometimes wear as bracelets."

The sole surviving male at the National Zoo is Hsing-Hsing, a name that refers to the twinkling of a star.

Submitted by Fred Beeman of Las Vegas, Nevada.

Why Don't Hand Dryers in Public Bathrooms Have an "Off" Switch or Button? And Why Does the Dryer Stay On for So Long?

❧ Before we get a pile of complaint letters, let us concede the point: Some automatic hand dryers *do* have an "off" switch. For example, Bobrick Washroom Equipment manufactures a model that does not have a separate "off" button but allows a user to push a button to turn it on and depress the same button a second time to shut it off. If you walk away after turning the dryer on, it shuts off automatically anyway, thirty seconds after it was first depressed.

But if you are talking about the genesis of hand-dryer conformation, then your discussion starts with World Dryer Corporation, a company that has dominated the field of automatic hand dryers in public bathrooms for more than forty-five years. We spoke to Linda Kilbryde, World's director of marketing, who told *Imponderables* that 95 percent of all public bathrooms in the U.S. still use paper towels. Of the remaining 5 percent that don't, Kilbryde claims that World has dryers in an astonishing 70 percent of them. And of course, many bathrooms use paper towels and automatic dryers.

Chances are, if you visualize a bathroom hand dryer, you are thinking of World Dryer's wall-mounted "Model A." As the name implies, World is still selling virtually the same design now that it did in 1941.

Why didn't the original hand dryer have an "off" switch? Kilbryde's opinion is that the simple one-button design was easier to execute, cheaper to manufacture, and more reliable. All of these advantages are exceedingly important, for World's competition has never been primarily other dryer manufacturers, but paper towels (and, earlier, cloth towel rolls). Therefore, anything that World can do to keep the price of the dryers low is crucial.

The price of a World Model A ranges between $350 and $400, obviously much more than a paper towel dispenser. But for a typical facility, the dryer will pay for itself in twelve to eighteen months; on a day-to-day basis, the electricity cost is but 10 percent of the costs of paper towels.

World also argues for the environmental advantages of electric dryers. Kilbryde cited an example: a typical fast-food restaurant. The average washroom might have approximately 50,000 hand dryings per year (140 per day—we hope a good percentage of those by employees). Each drying uses 2.5 paper towels, on average (in our experience, only about .5 of those towels ever actually comes in contact with hands). That adds up to 125,000 towels per year at a weight of 906 pounds. Installing an electric hand dryer in that rest room theoretically would save 7.7 trees per year, 1.4 cubic yards of landfill, and 9,065 gallons of water per year (each ton of paper production pollutes 20,000 gallons of water).

Dryers can save money in decreased plumbing bills (usually, damage as a result of paper-clogged sinks and toilets), in less labor for janitors in restocking dispensers, and cleanup from floors and sinks (indeed, we assume that many public buildings have banished paper towels completely in order to improve the appearance and cleanliness of their facilities). Furthermore, an electric dryer is available twenty-four hours a day, whereas paper towels can be depleted.

If an "off" switch were provided, the dryer would be subjected to persistent stop/start abuse that could stress the motor. One of the major selling points of the World Dryer is that a life of twenty to twenty-five years is not unexpected. In an age when electronics companies issue three-month warranties with a straight face, World stands behind a ten-year warranty with virtually no maintenance required by the buyer.

We couldn't help wondering, though, why hand dryers cycle on for a full thirty seconds. In our discussion of the bathroom habits of men and women in *How Does Aspirin Find a Headache?*, we noted that the average male retreats from the washroom with the alacrity of someone approached by an aluminum siding salesperson. Maybe women are different (Is that why women who go to the bathroom together are in there so long—are they bonding in front of hand dryers?), but from our casual observation, men wave their hands in front of hand dryers as if they were checkers scanning their hands at a grocery store checkout counter. It's fair to say that we've never seen a human being stand in front of a dryer for a full thirty seconds.

Kilbryde says that the thirty-second duration was chosen before the company first introduced the machines in the 1940s. "Real-life testing" was done by timing the "average dry time" and it was concluded that thirty seconds was the average time length required to accomplish the task "at hand." We have no doubt whatsoever that this much time is required, only that any human being has ever actually rubbed their hands together hard enough and long enough to achieve this arid state in a public bathroom.

But the times they are a-changing in the hand-drying industry. Increasingly, World, Bobrick, and other dryer companies are selling infrared machines, which contain sensors that detect the presence of hands placed in front of them (just as automatic sinks do). Alas, these machines save on electricity, just as the Model A saved paper. Although they cost more initially, the machines, at least if they prove as reliable as their predecessors, should save energy and money over the long run.

But the infrared machines not only have no "off" button, they have no "on" button.

Submitted by Susan Stock of Marlborough, Massachusetts.

David Feldman

Fig. 49. Subjects of groundbreaking 1962 "twin" study of mosquito attraction.

Why Do Mosquitoes Seem to Like Some People More Than Others?

☞ Of course, our correspondent was gracious enough to state her Imponderable delicately. Leslie really meant: "Why do mosquitoes *bite* some people more than others?" and, unless we're mistaken, even "Why do mosquitoes bite *me* more than others?"

As we learned in *Do Penguins Have Knees?*, only females bite us, for they need the protein in blood to sustain egg development. So it occurred to us that perhaps differences in human blood types might play a factor in mosquitoes' culinary preferences. Dr. Steven Schutz, of the University of California's Mosquito Control Research Laboratory, wrote us that although it was once believed that blood types were an important factor in varying attraction rates, this theory has been discredited.

And he concurred that Leslie is not paranoid:

> "Almost everyone who lives or works with mosquitoes has noticed that they seem to bite some people more than others. In part, this may be due to the fact that individual sensitivity to

mosquito bites varies among individuals, so some people notice bites more than others.

"However, it has been scientifically demonstrated that certain individuals are consistently more *attractive* to mosquitoes than others. . . . If you put two people in two different huts, one may consistently attract more mosquitoes than the other, and this pattern holds up in repeated trials.

"This does not necessarily mean the more attractive person will be bitten more; there are also preferences for biting different individuals, which may be independent of their long-range attractiveness."

The entomologists we contacted indicated that two of the factors that might influence biting behavior are heat and visual differentiation, as hard as they are to quantify. For example, Leslie Saul-Gershenz, insect zoo director of the San Francisco Zoological Society, says that *Aedes* mosquitoes seem to be attracted to warm bodies only when the temperature is below 15° Centigrade.

But almost certainly, the dominant factor in attracting mosquitoes is how you smell. We know that most mosquitoes are attracted to the odor of carbon dioxide, but all of us exude CO_2 every time we exhale, so that wouldn't explain why mosquitoes are attracted to particular individuals. Other smells are probably the determinants, possibly including lactic acid and octenol, two other chemicals that we know attract mosquitoes. And perhaps, mosquitoes are just as opinionated and arbitrary as we are, as Saul-Gershenz explains:

"We all smell a bit different, depending on our individual body chemistry. Just as we like some smells more than others, mosquitoes have very good chemoreception (sense of smell) and can detect these differences and express their preferences by feeding on some people more than others."

Schutz indicates that it is difficult to isolate particular components of insect attraction, and the solution to this mystery would be of help to more than authors of *Imponderables* books, for the answer might lead to better repellents and an ability to identify those most susceptible to mosquito-borne diseases, such as malaria.

Most insect repellents used by humans work on the principle of either masking odors that might attract mosquitoes or by creating smells that are repulsive. Randy Morgan, entomologist and head-keeper of the Insectarium at the Cincinnati Zoo, reports that

> ". . . regular intake of some materials (such as yeast), which ultimately are exuded through one's pores, change our smell and have proven effective in deterring mosquito bites."

On a personal and ironic note, Morgan reports that he, an entomologist, is far less attractive to mosquitoes than his wife, Kathy, who is a naturalist. He attributes this to her being "sweeter" than he is, but at best we're not sure this would bear the brunt of scientific rigor, and at worst this is a blatant attempt to butter up his spouse. And even though mosquitoes "reject" him, he can't take it personally: "My wife gets larger and more irritated welts from mosquitoes than I do."

Submitted by Leslie Alexander of Martin, North Dakota. Thanks also to Leslie Klein.

Frustables

❧ Admit it. We did a rather impressive job vanquishing those Imponderables, didn't we? Alas, we must remain humble, for the solution to other mysteries has eluded us.

We call these annoying conundrums "Frustables" (short for "Frustrating Imponderables") and we ask your help in providing solutions. Often, in the past, Frustables have been Imponderables that totally stymied us. This time around, we want to pose questions for which we think we have partial answers. Our expert sources propounded theories that we're not sure we buy. Let's see if you can do better than the experts.

We offer a complimentary autographed copy of our next *Imponderables* book to the reader who supplies the most convincing answer to each question, or the first reader who leads us to the proof that provides the solution. And your name will be emblazoned in the book, trumpeting your achievement. It's a tough job, but we're sure you're up to it.

Frustable 1: Why do we bite our fingernails?

Is this purely psychological? Could there be a physiological explanation? Biological? Anthropological? All we know is that oral manicures don't seem to be the best aesthetic solution, yet many are compelled to continue.

Frustable 2: Why do people feel the urge to urinate when they hear running water?

We have spoken to more urologists than you can shake a stick at, and we hear the refrain: "involuntary reflex." We'll accept that. But why? What biological function could this reflex serve?

Frustable 3: Why do many children tend to refuse to say "thank you" for gifts received, especially if their parents pressure them to express appreciation?

The child psychologists have differed in their answers to this question. Have you had an experience with this kind of behavior? What's your theory?

Frustable 4: Why do people tend to reposition their plates when served food?

Ever notice this behavior (which is probably unconscious)? Next time you are in a group at a restaurant, see how many folks move their plate, even if slightly, before actually touching the food. Any plausible explanation?

Frustable 5: Why do so many public buildings keep the internal temperatures so warm in the winter and so cold in the summer, particularly because this policy increases fuel bills during all seasons?

We would think that office buildings or movie theaters might tend to be a little chilly in the winter, but they always seem to be sauna-like. In the summer, they are like a meat locker. What's the deal?

Frustable 6: Why do bands in nightclubs always start performing late?

Is this a deliberate policy of club owners? Are bands in the dressing rooms ingesting controlled substances? Or tuning their instruments? Or combing their hair? Or dirtying their hair? Are customers invariably tardy and the clubs bowing to reality?

Frustable 7: Why is advanced math required in high school and college when many think that, say, geometry and calculus are irrelevant to their lives?

In an age of calculators and computers, many readers have posed this question as an Imponderable, wondering why anyone but aspiring mathematicians and scientists should be required to learn advanced math.

David Feldman

Frustable 8: Why do people put plastic deer ornaments on their front lawns?

Is this the icon of a strange cult? A totem of deer hunters? A substitute for jockey or pink flamingo lawn ornaments? Or do folks just think it looks purty?

Frustable 9: Why do construction workers soap the windows of retail stores when they are working inside?

Are they trying to keep us from looking in? If so, why? Are they trying to keep workers inside from looking out? If so, why? And are these the same folks who make us wonder about the Frustable below?

Frustable 10: Why do construction companies care so much if advertisements are posted outside their commercial construction sites? And why is the name of the architect and construction company usually listed, but not the name of the future tenant?

Construction companies (or their clients) seem so intent to keep posters from defacing the perimeter of their sites that they deface them themselves with omnipresent "Post No Bills" signs.

And why the obsession about withholding the name of the tenant of the new building or renovation?

Frustables Update

✌ **Our Readers Respond to the Frustables First Posed in** *How Does Aspirin Find a Headache?*

Frustable 1: Why Do We Close Our Eyes When We Kiss?

A paradox. This is one of the most frequently asked questions we receive; yet *Imponderables* readers seem to have strong feelings about the answer. Indeed, we received more mail about this Frustable than any of the others in this book. Perhaps we should set up a dating service to connect those who wonder about the answer with those who think they know the answer.

Most of you were adherents of one of three general theories:

The Focus Theory. Many readers mentioned that one of the nicest features about a kiss is that a good one can blot out a niggling distraction such as, say, reality. We are so bombarded with visual distractions in our everyday lives that it becomes a welcome relief to heighten other senses, as Paul Tang of San Diego, California, argues:

> "A kiss is not a visual activity to begin with: tactile, nasal, and oral sensations are emphasized. A friend even reports that the sloppy sounds of kisses can be stimulating. Having useless and disconcerting information coming in from one's eyes just takes away from the processing capacity of the brain. Closing one's eyes will free up the brain to savor the other inputs."

Many of you mentioned that you close your eyes during other wonderful sensual moments. Sondra Harris of West Haven, Connecticut, was typical:

> "I close my eyes while kissing for the same reason I close my eyes when enjoying any sublime sensation (a delightful odor, beautiful music, cheesecake—not fruitcake!)—in order to be as fully attuned to the sensation as possible, without interference from outside sources."

And, of course, kissing doesn't always take place in candlelit rooms with violins purring in the background. Still, we're not sure that reader Bill Gerk hasn't gone a little too far in his claims of the power of eye closure in blotting out some distractions:

> "If you're outside, you might worry about the torrential rainstorm, swarming bees or mosquitoes that are coming to greet you when your eyes are open while kissing. With your eyes closed, you won't concentrate on such bothersome annoyances until you complete your kissing or are actually interrupted by flooding, stinging, or puncturing (anaphylactic shock and lightning strikes are so rare that they seldom affect the way we osculate)."

Sheri Kimbrough and her husband offered several possible answers to this Frustable, though she seemed to side with the focus theory, herself:

"Closing your eyes intensifies the feeling. Since you don't generally close your eyes when you kiss your child, it seems likely. It's just a guess, but we sure had fun researching it!"

Hey, Sheri: anything for science.

The Cyclops Theory. A segment of readers thought the Focus Theory is just a tad pretentious. They were more concerned with a more mundane variety of focus—visual. Registered nurse Mardee Edelstein of Cortland, New York, states this theory succinctly:

"We close our eyes when we kiss because the distance between eye and kissee is too short to focus and is therefore uncomfortable. Our eyes close automatically when something comes *too* close—to protect them."

Or as Charles M. Wynn of Columbia, Connecticut, bluntly agrees: "Kiss a wall and you'll also close your eyes."

Many of you referred to this law of physics as a "Cyclops problem." Call her wacky, but Susan J. Barclay, of Sardis, British Columbia, would rather close her eyes than kiss a one-eyed man:

"Have you ever opened your eyes when kissing? Your partner looks very silly, almost like a Cyclops. It might turn off the average person if a lover looks like a mythical beast. If you have had fantasies of Ancient Greece this may be the proper course, but I personally find two-eyed men attractive."

There's no accounting for taste.

Many of you mentioned that in order to keep one's eyes open while kissing, it is necessary to "glaze" your eyes in order to prevent eyestrain. But some of you find "glazing" a superior alternative to enduring what the proponents of the third theory describe. . . .

The Fantasy Theory. We grow up with romantic images borrowed from movies, popular song lyrics, and our dreams. Occasionally our partners don't quite measure up to our aesthetic ideals. Alas, after the Focus Theory, it might be a tad deflating to read the following unsentimental treatise by Dallas Brozik of Huntington, West Virginia, a Frustable solver of long standing:

"Shakespeare was right when he said that the eyes are the window to the soul. You can see intelligence, stupidity, and fear just by looking deeply enough. That's why professionals engaged in contact sports watch each other's eyes rather than their biceps.

"Consider that romance is one of those human experiences that is shrouded in mystery. If you are really lucky, the person you are with may match the *a priori* image you hold in your mind. But most everybody realizes that everybody else is regrettably human and will never quite live up to all the fantasies.

"If you look the other person square in the eyes during a kiss, you *know* for sure that this is not exactly what you expected. By keeping your eyes closed, you maintain the mystery for a while longer, maybe even long enough for the other person to realize that you are not a total jerk and that you have some potential. Not only is ignorance bliss, it can be rather enjoyable at times, too."

Ignorance may indeed be bliss in this case. Your partner might be closing his or her eyes to avoid looking at your mug, but you can cling to the belief that the sole motivation is to intensify the ecstasy of your touch.

Lee Anne Hwang of Smyrna, Georgia, was a bit more prosaic than Brozik, but more graphic:

"You don't want to keep your eyes open and be forced to confront the huge, festering zit on the face of your beloved."

Reader Pamela R. Weiner of Kingston, New York, makes exactly the same point and adds,

"As we get older, our acne clears up but we keep that eye-closing habit."

And why were we not surprised when the answer we most feared came from a young woman, Rebekka Weinstein of Dallas, Texas?

"Why do you close your eyes when you kiss? So you can imagine that you're kissing someone else."

We did receive a few other random theories. One of the most intriguing came from Nancy Carr of Pittsburgh, Pennsylvania, who posited that for some people, closing the eyes might be

"a way of guarding against the intimacy of kissing. There's no chance for physical distance during a kiss, so closing the eyes may prevent a psychological barrier."

And several of you mentioned that you or a partner *do* keep your eyes open when you kiss. We had never even contemplated that there might be a gender-based distinction between men and women, but reader Lawren Ross Campbell E-mailed us cutting-edge research from the academic journal *Cosmopolitan.* An article quoted Andrew Stanway's book, *The Loving Touch:*

"Canadian anthropologist Pierre Maranda found that 97% of women keep their eyes closed when kissing, compared with only 30% of men. This does not mean that women are more likely to find their partner's looks unappealing—but that closed eyes allow them to fantasize while still enjoying the moment. Men, however, who are more visually stimulated, find that keeping their eyes open heightens their own desires."

Our favorite confirmation of this theory came from the same Sondra J. Harris we heard from earlier, who seems to be spending an *inordinate* amount of time ruminating about the implications of this

Frustable. Sondra's boyfriend, however, might be interested in a different kind of visual stimulation than Sondra has in mind:

> "During my extensive research while preparing to write this letter (should I apply for a grant?), I came across the astonishing fact that my boyfriend does *not* close his eyes while we are kissing. He says he likes to look at me while I am enjoying the kiss.
>
> "This led to more research (how dedicated I am!) where I tried opening my eyes mid-kiss. I agreed with him that watching is kind of nice, but I found my eyes closing involuntarily after just a few moments. . . .
>
> "My boyfriend may have placated me with his reason for kissing open-eyed, but I think the real cause for it is that he needs to keep an eye on the television."

As long as he has his hands on you instead of the remote control, Sondra, your relationship has hope.

Original Imponderable submitted by Leanne C. Collier of San Ramon, California. Thanks also to Gertrude Johnson of Clinton, Mississippi; Jennifer Morishima of Mercer Island, Washington; Mary Cannon of Chandler, Arizona; Kevin Coakley of Tallahassee, Florida; Deirdre Bradley of Gloucester, Massachusetts; Erin Anderson of Wentzville, Missouri; Ken Shafer of Traverse City, Michigan; Grace Weinstein of Los Angeles, California; and many others.

A complimentary book goes to Dallas Brozik of Huntington, West Virginia.

Frustable 2: Why Do Women "Of a Certain Age" Usually Start Wearing Their Hair Shorter?

If we received the most mail regarding the first Frustable, this one garnered the most theories. Often, one reader offered five or more different reasons to explain the incredible shrinking hair length on women.

Some of you provided a historical perspective. Judith Dahlman, of New York City, reminds us that before bobbed hair became the rage, current practices did not apply:

> "Prior to the 1920s, the average woman did not cut her hair. When she reached maturity, it was appropriate to either cover her hair completely or, in the nineteenth century, to wear it pinned up. I recall the four sisters in Louisa May Alcott's *Little Women*. The three older girls, all in their mid to late teens, wore their long hair in snoods. The youngest, still in school, wore hers long and free."

Is the change in style a response to physical changes in the hair structure? Some of you argued so, claiming that the thinness of

David Feldman

older hair is better disguised by shorter hairdos. We received such a personal testimony from Lois M. Cooper of Elma, Washington:

> "As a woman who recently entered that 'certain age,' I know I started wearing my hair short (after almost forty years of waist-length hair). As I got older, my hair lost body and sheen, became limp and dull, had split ends and just didn't look as pretty anymore."

When we were conducting research on this ourselves, many of the hairdressers we spoke to emphasized the changes not in the hair itself, but in the face and skin of women "of a certain age." Margaret Karmazin of Susquehanna, Pennsylvania, who proudly asserts that she is of "a certain age," files this report from the field:

> "As you age, everything on your face starts to drop lower. The nose drops, the cheeks sag, bags form under the eyes, the chin falls down, down, down. To counteract this, one needs the hair to direct the eyes away from this overall downward droop.
>
> "Hair cut to chin length or shorter lifts the eyes and gives an illusion of youthening the face. Picture an older, saggy face in the long, straight, parted-in-the-middle hairstyle of the early 70s (horrors!) and compare it to how a fresh young face would look with the same hairdo. The older woman would look like a witch or maybe a hillbilly.
>
> "Take the same older face and replace the 'do' with a short, upswept cut, maybe with some height on top, and you'll see a perked-up woman. Angela Lansbury on *Murder She Wrote* knows all the tricks. Of course, she's had face-lifts, but she also uses the short hair to give herself a breezy younger look."

Debra Allen, of Wichita Falls, Texas, makes the same point with a chilling bluntness:

> "By that certain age, you have probably begun to suspect that time and gravity are not friends. Your face somehow begins to

slide downward, until one day your jawline begins to remind you of Richard Nixon."

But many emphasized that short hair is simply easier and more convenient. As Denver, Colorado's, Joan Golden put it:

"I'm tired of spending an hour every morning doing my hair."

Nicole Coward of Wellington, Ohio, reports that she, her sister (who still sports longish hair), and her mother have all gone to shorter hair, simply for the sake of convenience:

"I am a twenty-year-old college student, and I recently had my hair, formerly shoulder-length, cut chin-length so that I don't have to deal with styling so much. Same story with my mother. In addition to working, cooking, helping my sister and me, and housecleaning, she is also supposed to spend upwards of a half hour styling her hair? No way!"

Several mentioned that as we get older and accumulate assorted aches and pains, especially arthritis, the lure of long hair seems increasingly resistible.

We were surprised how many tied the convenience factor to the birth of children. Some readers felt that the cutting of the hair is a sort of rite of passage, representing maturity and responsibility. Michelle Zimmerman of Fort Wayne, Indiana, puts a fascinating popular culture spin on this process:

"Speaking strictly from my own limited experience, the switch to shorter hair accompanied a major life change—childbirth. I no longer had the time or desire to fool around with long hair after the demands of taking care of a newborn rendered me sleepless and with less brainpower than before.

"My husband was quite chagrined when I had my hair cut, but he always had an image of me running through a field, my long hair blowing in the breeze, just waiting for him to catch

    David Feldman

me and lock in a passionate embrace. Come to think of it, this image probably precipitated the childbirth!

"It would seem that after childbirth, most women undergo a change in image, from the young innocent newlywed to the seasoned maternal type. Speaking from the vantage point of a mid-thirties memory (women of a certain age don't reveal their age, either), I remember that the matronly TV role models of my youth always had short hair—June Cleaver, Donna (Reed) Stone [we seem to remember her with longish hair during much of the run of the series], etc. The glamorous career women had long hair—Peggy Lipton of the *Mod Squad,* Barbara Eden (whose career was to be a genie), and Mary Tyler Moore during her show's first season.

"During the 1970s, as more and more women went to work and became 'liberated,' short haircuts became the norm, evidenced by Jane Fonda's shag hairstyle in *Klute* and the trendy wedge cut of Dorothy Hamill and Toni Tenille. Linda Evans had long hair when she played a ranch daughter in *The Big Valley,* but once she grew up and married Blake Carrington of *Dynasty,* she sported a shorter 'do.'

". . . Shorter hair represents a stepping-stone to Stage 2 of most women's lives, and after experiencing the ease of styling and caring for short hair, it's hard to go back to longer hair. Most men probably have no idea of the time and trouble that washing, curling, and styling long hair takes. I have seen a number of long-haired rock musicians of late, and I can't believe that any of those guys in the band Red Hot Chili Peppers prepares for a performance by wearing hot rollers for an hour or spending twenty minutes with a curling iron."

The advantages of short hair once you have babies is far more than symbolic, though. It can save on aspirin bills, as Evelyn Rosemore of Plano, Texas, explains:

"Babies pull, twist, and spit up on long hair, and it is easier to have hair that is out of a baby's reach."

One would think that by the time we are out of high school, we would become immune to the pernicious influence of peer pressure, but evidently the evil reach extends well into a "certain age." We received several letters that echoed Highwood, Illinois, Alice Conway's:

> "My hairdresser insisted on cutting my hair short. She said that older women look silly with longer hair, as if they were trying to pretend they were young.
>
> "My sister fought against this, but finally had to give in because the operator kept 'forgetting' and cutting her hair short."

But not just hair professionals apply the pressure. Our "old" pal Margaret Karmazin is fighting the good fight:

> "Let me state immediately that I myself am 'of a certain age' and that for reasons of vestigial rebelliousness, I refuse to join the masses and cut my hair short. I have hordes of friends working on me (it reminds me of *The Stepford Wives*) to cut my hair, but I steadfastly refuse."

Good for you.

Some readers wondered whether this peer pressure to cut hair as we get older is a way of venting our society's distaste for the linking of sexuality and advanced age. Ike House of Haughton, Louisiana, points out:

> "The vast majority of men I've talked to will readily admit long hair is much more attractive on women. However, after a woman is married, she doesn't want to attract attention from the opposite sex; that is, if she wants to *remain* happily married."

There is little doubt that long hair and sexuality are inextricably linked in American culture. One male reader named "Schiffman," who didn't supply us with his first name, thinks that "older women might have less need to use long hair as a 'mate attractor' if we're going to be Darwinian about this."

Not citing Darwin, our Gray Panther, Margaret Karmazin, unreluctantly agrees:

"Once a woman's biological clock has ticked down, she no longer has this intense urgency to pull in the opposite sex. Suddenly, after her raging sex hormones have quieted down, she sits up and realizes what a pain in the butt long hair was: 'What is this mess hanging down my back? It is annoying. It is hot. What am I doing with it??? Cut it off!!!' "

Even folks with raging hormones can find other advantages to short hair. Youngish Jeanne Salt of Tualatin, Oregon, has two young children and prefers the relatively carefree maintenance required to take care of her well-shorn tresses. Still, there are unexpected side benefits:

"My sweetheart is one of those rare men who prefers short hair. He claims it's because it is easier to nibble on my neck."

Original Imponderable submitted by Douglas Watkins, Jr., of Hayward, California. Thanks also to Crystal Moore of Salem, Illinois; Matt and George Schoendorff of Swartz Creek, Michigan; and Jenna Diotalevi of Milford, Massachusetts.

A complimentary copy goes to Margaret Karmazin of Susquehanna, Pennsylvania, to support her fight to quash peer pressure against long hair on women of a certain age.

Frustable 3: Why Do the Clasps of Necklaces and Bracelets Tend to Migrate From the Back Toward the Front?

First off, we are assuming that the posers of this Frustable were not referring to necklaces with big pendants or other heavy objects in the front. Such necklaces wouldn't have migrating clasps if they were engineered properly, as Kate Gladstone of Guilderland, New York, explains:

> "Necklace clasps pull forward because the heavy stuff in front levers them around. The heavier the clasp, the more it can act as a counterweight and stay put. Egyptian necklaces, for instance, had big, heavy, elaborate clasps in back."

Several correspondents argued that clasp migration can be traced directly to an annoying characteristic of humans: we move. Typical was Chris Avell of Arlington Heights, Illinois:

> "Humans, having no built-in shock absorbers, jolt their entire body when they walk. Every time we move we disturb the slumber of our jewelry.
>
> "The extra weight of the clasp pulling down on one side causes the jewelry to move in the same direction upon every disturbance.
>
> "Take into consideration that your neck and wrists are round, and anything unbalanced on something round tends to fall off. As one connected piece, the necklace or bracelet cannot fall off."

And what direction will it move? Sir Isaac Newton had a theory about this. He called it "gravity." Reader Dallas Brozik of Huntington, West Virginia, elaborates:

> "The reason that necklace clasps migrate from the back to the front is gravity. Gravity is an insidious force that tries to make all objects inside a particular gravity well arrange themselves so that they have a minimum of potential energy.
>
> "As an experiment, fill a box with different-sized marbles composed of the same material (so that they have the same unit density), and then agitate the box. The smaller marbles, which are lighter, will wind up on the bottom while the larger, heavier marbles will wind up on top. Gravity causes the marbles in the box to find the configuration with the lowest over-

all potential energy, which means that all the space at the bottom of the box will be more tightly filled, even if it is with smaller, light marbles.

"The necklace phenomenon is analogous. The clasp on most necklaces is often larger than the chain, and even if it is about the same size it has a different shape, usually with square corners. If a necklace is put on with the clasp at the back, every motion of the head and neck will cause the clasp to move against the skin. While this motion will always occur, it is exacerbated if the clasp is under clothing so that it can be caught between skin and fabric.

"As a person makes normal head motions, the clasp will crawl up one side of the neck until it is over the shoulder line and passes to the front. Once in front, the clasp is usually free of the fabric (remember that the chain is worn in order to be seen), and it will continue to fall down the gravity well until it gets as low as possible, which is the front-bottom of the chain."

Not all clasps are symmetrical, though, and Larry J. Van Stone of Stillwater, Oklahoma, believes that these irregularities can affect the movement:

"Bodily motions that cause the chain to slide a little bit are resisted in one direction and not the other, so the clasp creeps around."

A few readers took us to task for presuming a phenomenon that doesn't even exist. Brenda Barrise of Phoenix, Maryland, concedes that our regular movements would move the clasp, but that doesn't mean that we have proven any principle of physics, and certainly not that the clasp was in any way responsible for the movement:

"The clasp is a break in the uniform pattern of the necklace or bracelet that acts as a type of 'marker' that we can use to see if its position has changed. Imagine a gold chain that has no clasp and looks exactly the same all around. It could turn a thousand times and we might never notice because there is no reference point, for every part of the gold chain looks exactly the same."

Want to know why we spent much of our academic career ducking science classes? Maybe because we were afraid of encountering a professor like Christopher Bauer of the University of New Hampshire, who would question our half-baked theories and assumptions. Bauer writes:

"There are several possibilities—all tentative hypotheses that could be resolved via controlled experiment and good record-keeping. But no one ever does that." [Do we smell a science fair project brewing?]

"To be fair, you should ask: Do necklaces and bracelets put on *backwards* tend to migrate into the proper alignment? But no one ever starts from this position. If the necklace is fairly uniform in size and mass all the way around, the normal jostlings of movement would cause random motion of the necklace so that regardless of the initial position, the jewelry could end up in many other positions over time.

"How many people get upset when their necklace is found to be in the *right* location? Of course, no one bothers to remember these unnoteworthy events. We only tend to take note of the unusual. 'I was just thinking about you when you called!' How many times were you thinking about that person when there was *no* call?"

Makes sense, Professor Bauer, although we'd like you to meet Grace B. Weinstein, of Los Angeles, California, who reports a phenomenon stranger than fiction:

"The ring on my left hand always migrates to the left and the ring of my right hand always migrates to the right. It can't be the rotation of the earth, because that would make both rings migrate in the same direction. As the King of Siam said, 'Is a puzzlement!' "

David Feldman

Original Imponderable submitted by Stephanie Singer of Santa Cruz, California. Thanks also to Ed Hawkins of Kathleen, Georgia; and Laura Schisgall and Margaret Ball of New York, New York.

A complimentary book goes to Christopher Bauer of Newmarket, New Hampshire.

Frustable 4: Why Is It Customary to Include the Full Address of the Recipient of a Business Letter Before the Salutation?

In *How Does Aspirin Find a Headache?*, we mused that the recipient of a letter presumably knows his or her address. We assumed that this custom was an unnecessary relic of the days when typewriters were king and the recipient's address was typed to fit into the transparent slot in window envelopes.

"Wrong!" blared *Imponderables'* readers. And you've convinced us that there are solid reasons to continue this heretofore puzzling practice:

1. **It's for the sender's benefit.** The strongest and most often cited advantage was typified by this letter from Reverend J. Stewart Culkin, Pastor of Saint Mark's Catholic Church in Vienna, Virginia:

> "The full address of the recipient is put on a business letter above the salutation not for the recipient, who should know his address, but for the correspondent who normally keeps a copy of the letter to reference subsequent correspondence.
>
> "For example, I have included your return address on this letter because I shall pass your delightful book on to someone else [If it was so delightful, how could you bear to part with it?]. Therefore a copy of this letter in my computer (no more carbon copies, thank goodness) will be my only record of your address."

Several readers focused on the convenience of this arrangement. Bill Jelen of Akron, Ohio (remember that name, you are going to be reading many of his theories), anticipated one of our possible objections:

> "Most businesspeople keep a file of their outgoing correspondence. Since the sender doesn't have a copy of the envelope, it provides a record of the receiver's address.
>
> " 'But wait,' you say, 'if you have the address initially, why don't you just keep it in the Rolodex instead of duplicating it?' Insurance. The Rolodex could be stolen, lost, or cleaned out. At least if the letter survives, you will have a copy of the address."

Several readers, such as Murray Beauchamp of Winnipeg, Manitoba, admitted that they were too lazy to file most letters:

> "If you are like me, you never file the copy; you just shove it somewhere on the desk. Then when you want to write to them again (to ask why they haven't responded yet), you don't have to look up the address; just find the copy.
>
> "Now of course if you are going to write to them again, you don't need to do this. For example, I'm never going to write to you again, so look what's at the top of this letter!"

You guessed it: a gaping hole where our address should be.

2. **The Post Office Theory.** Actually, Bill Jelen refers to this as the "Destroyed Envelope Theory":

> "Back in the days of the pony express, it was probably a lot more likely that the envelope would become obliterated en route. Thus, by including a copy of the address inside, there was still a chance the mail would arrive at its intended address. Come to think of it, the same reason could help the dead-letter people in modern mail delivery."

And Jerry Borths of Charlevoix, Michigan, was the first of several readers to mention that if the address on the outside of the envelope was smeared or illegible, the post office could open up the envelope and send the letter to its proper destination.

3. Routing. Misdirection isn't confined to the postal system, however. Bobbie Holz of Parma, Ohio, writes:

> "We need that address. As an employee of a Fortune 300 company with about 15 plants and 20,000 employees in North America, I can answer this one very easily. If a letter comes to our CEO, 99 times out of 100 the letter really shouldn't have to come to him. So he routes it to who he thinks should get it, which 99 times out of 100 still isn't the right person. So that person routes it to who he or she thinks should get it and the odds improve a little bit.
>
> "Sometimes these letters jump from plant to plant to headquarters to Canada back to the U.S. By the time the person who should really get the correspondence gets the letter it has been routed to a bazillion people who have all scribbled on it and said, 'Let me know what happens with this. Bill.'
>
> "Give me a break. There are 92,000 'Bills' in our company. How can I follow up if I have no idea who the letter originally went to?"

4. Typists. Alfonso F. del Granado of Chicago, Illinois, writes:

> "The writer of the letter is often not the one who mails it—that job may go to the secretary or assistant. The secretary would then find it useful to have the address already on the letter, instead of having to turn to the Rolodex. The address may also be non-standard, different from the one on file. If things are busy or disorganized, the letter may sit around awhile, or even be lost in the shuffle."

Furthermore, with the dominance of word processors in most offices, this custom that started with typewriters proves particularly handy with cyber-software. Charles Kluepfel of Bloomfield, New Jersey, explains:

"In the case of a word processor, you don't need a Rolodex or address book, or even address-book software. Just pull up the last letter that you wrote to the recipient. It has the address in it."

5. The cc Theory. Bill Jelen notes that if a letter is copied to a third party, that person would now have a record of both the sender and receiver's addresses. Jelen admits that to put all parties on an equal footing, we should probably state the full address of all the people who are cc'd, as well.

6. The Style Manual Theory. Bill notes that anyone who takes a typing class or consults a style manual will be taught to include the recipient's full address above the salutation. So more than one generation is "just following orders."

7. The Same Reason We Have a Last Name Theory, aka The Posterity Theory. Once again, we yield the floor to Bill Jelen:

"If I just started this letter, 'Dear Dave,' that might mean nothing to me ten years from now. Dave Who? Dave Barry? My Uncle Dave? The address conveys a lot of information. I get the receiver's full name, his title, and who he works for.

"Thus ten years from now I will know I wrote to Joe Smith, manager of quality control for the Fozboz Computer Company. This is a lot more helpful than seeing that I wrote to Joe or Joe Smith."

Original Imponderable submitted by Darrel Elmore of Miami, Florida. Thanks also to Robert Grosek of Binghamton, New York.

A complimentary book goes to Bill Jelen of Akron, Ohio.

David Feldman

Frustable 5: Why Do Most Women Like Shopping More Than Men?

As we reread this Frustable, we were gratified that no females misinterpreted its meaning. After all, we were inquiring about why more women than men seem to prefer shopping, not why more women seem to prefer shopping to men. We shudder contemplating what the reaction would have been to *that* question.

Your response to this Frustable surprised us. We expected primarily psychological explanations, but instead we were deluged with anthropological and genetic theories. Fifteen-year-old Dominik Halas of Oakville, Ontario, thinks the roots of our shopping differences leans back to personkind's earliest days:

> "As any anthropologist will tell you, in primitive societies, men filled the role of hunter and women that of gatherer. This explains this discrepancy in the shopping habits of men and women.
>
> "Men, being hunters, would go out in search of one object: meat. Since most mammals are equally edible, they would probably attack the first easy target they found. Since an animal might last for several days as food, they would immediately go home. . . . Today's men, who no longer have to hunt, still buy the first of anything that they find.
>
> "Women, on the other hand, would search for a much wider variety of foods, which would change seasonally, and even from day to day. Being confronted with a wide variety of berries, nuts, and roots, they would have to be selective, taking the time to pick the berries or dig up the roots only if they had the greatest nutritional value. Often they would come by an edible plant by chance. Thus modern women visit many different stores and spend so much time looking around at the various items—it's a throwback to primitive times."

Another young reader, Daria Ovidé, a high-school sophomore from Dayton, Ohio, notes that although the male hormone testosterone might have propelled primitive men to hunt, women also have some testosterone in their systems:

> "This gives women the need to hunt in some manner. A feminine form of hunting may be shopping. The small amount of testosterone propels women to hunt, while the estrogen determines what they hunt."

While reading Jane Auel's books (e.g., *Clan of the Cave Bear*), John M. Sullivan of Mineola, New York, was also struck by the correlations between cavemen as hunters and cavewomen as gatherers with shopping preferences in contemporary life:

> "Translated into today's shopping malls, women will stop and browse at every counter of every store looking to see what might be nice, while men, shopping for shoes, for instance, will not even glance at another item. They could be selling $400 suits for $5 and a man 'hunting' for shoes will not even notice. Thus while men's hunting and gathering applies to very specific items, women will look at every 'plant' in the field looking for a nice pair of earrings."

Bob Kowalski of Detroit, Michigan, notes that the single-mindedness of men makes coed trips to a mall annoying for both parties: "Women go shopping, while men go buying!"

In other words, men tend to be goal-oriented. Reader Joan Golden of Denver, Colorado, points out that there are social dimensions for women in shopping that are not important, or even desirable, to men:

> "Women enjoy going 'into the marketplace,' to be where the other people are and to see what's new, ask questions, and make the purchase from another person. Men would be just as happy getting stuff delivered, as long as they don't have to talk to the delivery person."

David Feldman

We think Golden is onto something with this social dimension. For although all the foregoing theories help explain why women might be compelled to browse, it doesn't explain their *enjoyment* of shopping. Women seem much happier "gathering" in stores than men do "hunting" their purchases.

Debra Allen of Wichita Falls, Texas, emphasizes the importance of sociability in women's enjoyment of shopping:

"To most men, shopping means 'you need a specific item, you find it, you buy it, you're done, you go home.' To most women, however, shopping is more of a social outing that may or may not involve buying anything. Friction seems inevitable, doesn't it? It's like a track meet where one team came prepared for a marathon and the other for the 50-yard dash. As for why shopping is so often the social outing of choice?

"1. Shopping is a good excuse to visit with each other while accomplishing something. It's the modern version of quilting bees.

"2. Between a job and the housework which, let's be honest, boys, women usually do the lioness's share of, the only way you have time to see your friends sometimes is to combine shopping and visiting. Plus, necessity shopping (groceries, kids' clothing, etc.) tends to be dull and company helps break up the monotony.

"3. If you meet at someone's house to visit, then they have to do more housework, which kills the point of getting a break.

"4. Most of us don't have tons of cash on hand for entertainment and the mall is free. Window shopping, at most, costs the price of lunch or, if you're really strapped, a Coke. And if you have to, you can take the kids."

Allen mentions the social factors primarily as a refuge from what could otherwise be drudgery. But there is an aesthetic dimension to shopping that women seem to enjoy much more than men. Even Debra Allen reports: "We just like to look at pretty things!" A more passionate proponent of the aesthetic theory is Lee Anne Hwang of Smyrna, Georgia:

"Women like things to look nice; men like things to *work* nice. Men tend to concentrate on the functionality and comfort of a garment, but women hang around the store considering whether they can wear it without looking fat, if they have anything that goes with it, and if they'll need a new pair of shoes for it.

"Women like to picture how everything *looks* together. This goes for things like curtains and furniture, too. I have a single male friend who recently bought a house. He plans to install off-white miniblinds all over the house. I suggested fabric or pleated shades or perhaps drapes or curtains, and he grimaced.

" 'Curtains are a *girl* thing,' he told me. 'Miniblinds work well enough for me. They do the job.'

"The upshot of all this is that it is less fun to shop if you aren't interested in store displays of bishop-sleeve drapes and just want to find off-white miniblinds than if you're standing there musing pleasurably whether fabric shades and a valance or tab-top curtains would go best with what you have, and what you still have to buy to make it all look really good."

Zzzzzzzzzzzzzz.

Whoops. We nodded off there for a second.

When we first posed this Frustable, we noted that we were aware that the assumption implied in the sexual divide was a gross generalization. Even so, one reader, Helen Stranzl of Ste. Dorothee, Quebec, questioned the validity of the stereotype. She notes that most malls consist of female-oriented shops:

"Have you ever seen three hardware stores, a few motorcycle shops, car dealerships, and sports stores all under one roof? If you were to put all these stores in one building and call it a shopping mall, how many women would you expect to see?

"Women would be crowding the benches and having anxiety attacks trying to think of how much more time it will take before they could rest their tired feet on the couch at home with a nail file in one hand and a Diet Coke in the other, watching their favorite soap operas.

". . . Besides, women are forced to do the shopping. Could you imagine what North America would look like if the men shopped for their own clothes? Please, I'd rather never find out the answer to that Imponderable."

A complimentary book goes to Debra Allen of Wichita Falls, Texas.

Frustable 6: How and Why Did the Association Between Wearing Eyeglasses and Nerdiness and/or Intelligence Begin?

Many readers framed the stereotype as a by-product of traditional sex roles that are inflicted upon children at a young age. Angela Stockton of Clermont, Florida, makes a strong argument for this proposition:

> "Instead of 'What does a person look like if he wears glasses?' and answering 'a nerd,' ask 'What does a person *not* look like if he wears glasses?' The answer, of course, is 'a jock.' Before contact lenses, no schoolboy with poor eyesight played sports beyond what was required in P.E. So if a boy couldn't compete in athletics, the only field in which he could compete was academics.
>
> "Unfortunately, the first ambition of every boy is to be a sports hero, not a Rhodes scholar. Thus the jock is admired, and the nonjock cruelly labeled a nerd. Significantly, you never hear a girl called a nerd because, at least until Title IX, girls were not encouraged to play sports. If they did anyway, they were called 'tomboys,' and *that* was an insult. More significantly, when a coach tries to motivate a male athlete through

shame, he will typically call him a 'sissy' or worse, or sneer that he kicks/throws/shoots/runs/bats (whatever) 'like a girl.' "

Joe Williams of Chireno, Texas, adds that as children, many who wore glasses avoided sports and fights to prevent breaking their glasses or to avoid damaging them, and their non-four-eyed friends were issued warnings:

> "Also, boys were instructed not to hit people with glasses on. All this gave the impression of sissiness or nerdiness on the part of the glasses-wearers."

Linden Malki of San Bernardino wonders if sports-minded children would notice vision problems as much as "bookworms" and therefore might not be diagnosed as early as bookworms:

> "The stereotype could also have come about because most older people need glasses, and a connection is made between young people with glasses and older, sedentary and unhip adults."

And although it has been disproven that excessive reading causes myopia in children, this myth has persisted. Now most children with vision problems are diagnosed and given glasses, if needed. But Douglas Shaver of Jacksonville, Florida, points out that this wasn't always the case, and that bookworms were the most likely to obtain and use eyeglasses:

> "During most of the time since glasses were invented, the only people likely to be wearing them would be those whose customary activities would have been difficult or impossible without normal vision, and in low-tech societies there don't happen to be many such activities. Unless a person's vision is extremely defective, he or she can learn to manage rather well at just about anything.
> "Among the exceptions, and the one relevant to this dis-

cussion, is reading. When glasses are a luxury, those who wear them are likely to be reading a lot of books.

"Even in modern times the stereotype is often manifest among children in schools serving disadvantaged communities. Many children who should be wearing glasses may not have them unless their parents are sensitive to the importance of intellectual achievement. In such communities, the kid with glasses is, again, likely to be a bookworm."

But one school of readers came up with a novel theory: Perhaps this stereotype persists because it is true! Reader Donna Phillips of Catlin, Illinois, was kind enough to send us an article, "Smart Looks," written by Bruce Goldman, published in the July/August 1989 issue of *Hippocrates*. In this article, Goldman cites several studies that indicate:

• A disproportionately high percentage of lawyers, doctors, and academics are myopes.
• A study of 150,000 male Israeli army recruits indicated that soldiers with the highest IQs and superior formal education were most likely to be myopic. Furthermore, 27 percent of the recruits with IQs above 128 were myopic, while only 8 percent of those with IQs below 80 were.
• Among a sampling of seventh-graders who were given the SAT test, 55 percent of the children who did "exceptionally well" on either the math or verbal sections were nearsighted.

Goldman then speculates about what might cause these distinctions. One possibility is that myopic kids are physically incapable of attaining superiority in sports that rely upon hand-eye coordination, so therefore apply themselves to reading. But a British study found not only that nearsighted children played outside as much as their normal-sighted counterparts, but were superior readers before the onset of myopia.

So Goldman concludes that heredity is likely to play a factor:

David Feldman

"University of Minnesota psychologist Thomas J. Bouchard, Jr., who studies pairs of twins raised apart, says: 'If two identical twins walk in here wearing glasses, they can typically exchange them and see very well.' Studies by Bouchard and others suggest that mental ability—or at least whatever it is that intelligence tests measure—is also carried in the genes. When two inherited traits cluster together statistically, researchers are tempted to ask whether they're somehow genetically linked. A gene partly responsible for intelligence could travel on the same chromosome as a gene affecting eyesight, for example."

Original Imponderable submitted by Bruce Kershner of Williamsville, New York. Thanks also to Colleen Ho of Rockville, Maryland; Matt and George Schoendorff of Swartz Creek, Michigan; Franchetta Smith of Orlando, Florida; Matt Conrad of Bloomington, Indiana; Jennifer Rosen of Chicago, Illinois; and Kathleen Kuo of Aiea, Hawaii.

A complimentary book goes to Donna Phillips of Catlin, Illinois.

Frustable 7: Why and Where Did the Tradition of Tearing Down Football Goalposts Begin?

If we had to name a King of Frustables, it would have to be reader Bill Gerk of Burlingame, California, who attempts to solve every Frustable in every *Imponderables* book. Bill claims that this Frustable is the most difficult we have ever posed. And he was a little annoyed that the "where" component of this mystery violates one of our definitions of an Imponderable as stated in *Why Do Dogs Have Wet Noses?* ("They are 'why' questions rather than who/what/where/ [when] trivia questions"):

"Still, it's your book. You are the one who coined and discovered *Imponderables* and Frustables. I can't sue and recover. I can't have you jailed. So, all I can do is get it off my chest in polite words—seeking to avoid the pettiness of suggesting I beat this Frustable because I caught you thumbing your nose at one of your own criteria.

"I could bluff on the 'where' part with the pretense that I'm a centenarian who participated in the original tearing down of football goalposts while in attendance at Hiram Slick University in Punkin Crick, Iowa. That the local paper had a long feature article about our starting the tradition of tearing down football goalposts in 1912. That, unfortunately, no copies of this feature article are extant.

"But as Mark Twain said, 'I'm better than George Washington. I can tell a lie but won't lie.' "

So Bill applied himself and attempted to answer this Frustable the old-fashioned way: with research. Bill found the earliest reference to goalposts in *Famous First Facts,* written by Joseph Nathan Kane. The book states

"that football goalposts were used in the contest between McGill University (Montreal, Canada) and Harvard University played at Cambridge, Massachusetts, May 14, 1874."

Before goalposts, goals were scored by kicking the ball across the goal line (see our discussion of the evolution of American football in *Why Do Dogs Have Wet Noses?*)—the forward pass wasn't legalized until 1906. But there is no evidence that these goalposts were defaced in any way, let alone torn down.

Gerk persisted in his digging, however, and unearthed other references to the tearing down of goalposts in the late nineteenth and early twentieth centuries. In his book *Sports Spectators* (Columbia University Press, 1986), Alan Guttman describes the fan mania that engulfed Ivy League football by the end of the nineteenth century. Perhaps because they were the children of the privileged, loutish fan behavior was indulged:

". . . violence became a problem: but it was the violence on the field that worried observers, not the violence of the spectators, whose whoops and cries and drunken revelry were grudgingly accepted as youthful (i.e., tolerable) exuberance. . . . The undergraduates were expected to 'let off a little steam' and to tear down an occasional goalpost. The police took little note of their behavior."

We were particularly smitten by this more specific account of fan violence from the turn of the century. Perhaps sociologists and pundits who think boorishness is a modern-day invention might be interested in perusing this account by Gilda Berger in her 1990 book, *Violence and Sports*, published by Franklin Watts:

> "One particularly long-lasting and rough rivalry exists between the students of the Colorado School of Mines and those at Colorado College. Since 1899, there has been tremendous tension at the annual game held by the two teams.
>
> "In the old days, the winners would celebrate victory by using dynamite to blow up the rival's goalposts. And it was an act of uncommon bravery for a Colorado College student to venture anywhere near the School of Mines. It has been said that any Mines students who caught a Colorado College guy on campus during the week before the game would burn an M on the forehead with nitric acid."

Luckily, most colleges *aren't* mining schools, so fans have traditionally resorted to brute force. Ray Schmidt, a leading researcher of college football, told *Imponderables* that the early goalpost-tearing involved fans of victorious visiting teams defacing the symbol of the home team's territory. What would motivate fans to uproot goalposts? We received a witty response from Bob Carroll, of the Pro Football Research Association:

> "I can't pinpoint the time or place, although it obviously started back when goalposts were made of wood. It's undoubtedly related to the warfare practice of taking a trophy (i.e., scalp, finger, virgin) from a vanquished foe, and *that* started before recorded history.
>
> "Do the losers ever tear down goalposts? Did the losers ever take scalps? You can picture an ebullient crowd intoxicated with victory looking around for something to take home

to remember the moment. Well, the winning team had the ball. And the losing team protected their jerseys (and lives) by getting the hell out. What was left? The goalposts!

"It was the perfect answer. Not only could goalposts be broken into little pieces so that everyone could have a piece—kind of like medieval pilgrims who grabbed every splinter somebody said came from the True Cross—but also when the moment faded in bleak December, you could toss it on the fire to warm up your living room.

"Maybe some deep psychological quirk in *Homo americanus footballus* makes a religious connection with the goalpost. Or perhaps the primitive need for warmth brings out a sublimated wood-gathering instinct. Or possibly the violent buffeting during the game leads even the most milquetoasty to crave a frenzied climax to the day's celebration. Or could it be that a couple of guys just needed some lumber to repair the outhouse roof? It makes one ponder."

Reader Jimmy Stephens of Richmond, Virginia, was kind enough to pass along a wonderful essay by folklorist Alan Dundes that we had read in college. The chapter "Into the Endzone for a Touchdown: A Psychoanalytic Consideration of American Football" can be found in Dundes's book *Interpreting Folklore*. Dundes argues that everything in football, from its terminology to its uniforms, is replete with sexual and homoerotic overtones. The chapter is a *tour de force*, and we will let interested readers decide on their own whether the fact that all the major team sports involve one side trying to violate an opponent's territory has the significance ascribed by a certain Viennese psychiatrist:

"It does not require a great deal of Freudian sophistication to see a possible sexual component in such acts as throwing a ball through a hoop, hitting a puck across a 'crease' into an enclosed area bounded by nets or cage, and other structurally similar acts."

Dundes notes that coaches incite their players by using rape metaphors, and Stephens speculates that the tearing of goalposts might be, at least in part, a symbolic gang rape of the vanquished foes (and their fans).

Reader Bill Jelen notes that similar rituals can be found in other sports. At the end of the NCAA basketball finals or the end of most tournaments, a player from the winning side cuts down the net. And after the final game in Municipal Stadium, the home plate of the Cleveland Indians was dug up. Jelen continues:

> "I can understand the net will probably end up in someone's trophy room. The Indians' home plate is going to Cooperstown. But what the heck do the people do with the [metal] goalpost once they get it out of the parking lot?"

A complimentary book goes to Bill Gerk of Burlingame, California.

Frustable 8: Why Do Artists, Models, and Bohemians Wear Black Clothing?

We're not entirely convinced by the responses to this Frustable. As we discussed in *How Does Aspirin Find a Headache?*, a black outfit seems to be an enduring "uniform" among the trendy, yet many of the arguments proffered for wearing black would apply to accountants and file clerks as well as artists and models.

Dallas Brozik, who is of Bohemian ancestry rather than a bohemian lifestyle, reminded us that the original purpose of many black uniforms was strictly practical:

> "a lot of people wore dark clothes because black did not show dirt (professors' robes are black so as not to show soot from candles and lamps)."

Mardee Edelstein of Cortland, New York, amplifies:

> "Artists' garrets didn't have bathrooms or fine beds, maybe not even good heat, and people in the throes of creative and artistic passion were presumed not to take time for such mun-

dane things as changing clothes, washing, undressing at night, and so on."

We couldn't help but marvel how readers were arguing both sides of the fence. Some of you maintain that a black outfit makes the wearer stand out from the crowd; others that it helps the bohemian to blend into the crowd. Reader Joan Golden notes that the artist Georgia O'Keeffe once remarked that

> "bright or stylish clothing would have distracted her visually from what she was trying to express on canvas. Wearing simple, black clothing kept her focused."

Some of you attempted to reconcile the conflicting strains of conformity and nonconformity. Says Dallas Brozik:

> "So what is a good antisocial type supposed to do to make a statement? Loud, garish clothing is 'in,' so you must wear black, a color associated mostly with funerals in the Western world. Besides, wearing black probably serves as a tribal marker for those folks (consider the black leathers worn by motorcycle types). Everybody has to be different in one way or another; clothing is the easiest."

Craig Kirkland, a violist who often must wear all-black outfits when performing, compares this custom to the Frustable we once posed about why so many policemen wear mustaches:

> "Artists are all a little different, and wearing black can be like saying, 'I'm different, but in a particular way that stands out but which others share.' "

Kirkland points out that for many models and performance artists, black is the most practical color. Black photographs better with black-and-white film than other colors, and reflects less light. Technical and crafts specialists in the arts often wear black, as well, in order to *not* be noticed during a performance. When playing in an orchestra pit during an opera, Kirkland points out that musicians are often asked to wear all-black,

> "because we aren't supposed to be seen. We aren't, unless people gawk over the pit like we're zoo animals."

But no one compels bohemians to wear black when not working, and any trip to a SoHo coffeehouse will reveal that artists and models wear black during their off time, too. Reader Debra Allen recognizes the paradox of "attention-seeking" people who

> "catch the eyes of others while at the same time announcing that they are above the boorish tyranny of fickle fashion. As for punksters, black doesn't distract your attention from their, um, statement."

Or as Mardee Edelstein summarizes:

> "Plain black also lets the world know that you are renouncing 'style' for deeper values of substance. . . ."

And what might that substance be? Why, *angst,* of course! Several of you commented that black is the color of mourning and associated with death, and thus the best hue to convey the soul-satisfying alienation of the artistic soul. We loved this explanation of Pam Matthews of Reading, Pennsylvania:

> "Among the artsy, being full of angst and nihilistic depression is *good.* Black embodies all the sorrows of our world. It's the color of mourning. Black absorbs all other colors. Black can be seen as the absence of color, which makes it just the kind of statement a Sartre-reading kind of person would be 'into.'
>
> "But I think the true reason why Bohemian types wear black, black, and more black is that it makes a profound statement of cynicism and negativism and reinforces the whole nonreality of everything.

"I once aspired to artsiness, but became a librarian instead."

So we guess you have a few other colors represented in your closet, Pam.

Maybe we haven't found a definitive answer here. Maybe there isn't one. Craig Kirkland even took the initiative to pose this Frustable to three musician friends who habitually wear all-black. This was the response:

> "Musician A: 'I like the way I look in black.'
> "Musician B: 'I'm depressed a lot.'
> "Musician C: 'Black hides stains and it's easy to wash and nobody will think I'm someone else because everyone knows I always wear black.'
> "Maybe we're back at square one."

Exactly.

A complimentary book goes to Craig Kirkland of Greenville, North Carolina.

Frustable 9: Why Is the Best Restaurant Coffee Better Than Home-Brewed Coffee?

Families have been riven over coffee conflicts, so we expected a little more passion about this Frustable. Surprisingly, only a few of you grumbled about the basic premise. Strongest in her dissent was Mardee Edelstein of Cortland, New York:

> "I think it all tastes like poison. If you watch the commercials, apparently the very *best* restaurants have been chosen to have their coffee thrown out and a certain brand of instant coffee substituted with not a single patron knowing anything more than that the coffee is better than ever that night. Or so they say."

Actually, all the theories posited by readers fell into two camps: psychological and technical. The psychological faction argues that the superior taste of restaurant coffee can be ascribed to the pleasure of expectation. As Bill Gerk put it:

> "Most people do not dine out routinely. So when they do, they look forward to it. They expect the chefs to produce savory and succulent foods that surpass their amateurish efforts. This pleasurable expectation carries over to the coffee."

But most of you argued that just about *anything* tastes better when you don't have to prepare it yourself. Haughton, Louisiana, dentist Ike House theorizes:

> "The main reason is that we don't have to fix it and we don't have to clean it up. This ability to relax and enjoy could show that it is not that the coffee tastes better, we just appreciate it more."

We're not sure we buy these contentions. Sure, not having to slave over a hot stove is always a treat, but it seems to us that most folks are willing to carp about restaurant food and drink. It seems to us that high expectations might make it harder for restaurant fare to please us.

Neil Parker of Summerland, British Columbia, who used to work in the coffee industry, offers a few of the technical advantages a restaurant java might have over a home brew:

> "One has to do with the equipment restaurants use: the flow-through drip machines with carafes. Although arguably better than other systems, they have the advantage of not boiling the water as many home coffeemakers do (boiling renders the water too hot for proper coffee making).
>
> "Another reason is volume. Coffee is better made fresh, and restaurant coffee is used up quickly and made fresh more often than at home. Because of this, a restaurant can often use

David Feldman

milder, more aromatic beans that go bitter more quickly if left on a hot burner.

"Cleanliness. In good restaurants, it is somebody's job to properly clean the coffeemakers and carafes (often at home, the carafe is simply rinsed out and baskets are rarely cleaned). When I worked for Diplomat Coffee Services, the cleanliness of the machines was the biggest source of customer dissatisfaction with coffee taste."

Obviously, some restaurants also use superior coffee to brands we might buy for home use, but the premise of this Frustable assumes that the coffee quality is equal. Still, other ingredients can be a factor. Parker solved an Imponderable of his own, recently. He couldn't figure out why his cup of coffee at Tim Horton's Donut Shop tasted better than the same coffee taken home. Was it because of the psychological lift provided by the charming ambience at Tim's? Nope, Neil discovered:

"I have just found out that Tim Horton's uses 18 percent cream instead of the 10 percent light cream that I use myself."

Jane Sekerak of Venetia, Pennsylvania, posed this Frustable to the folks at her favorite coffee emporium, The Coffee Beanery. They noted that they used purified water, important in places with poor tap water, but also attributed much of their quality to cleaning the brewing machines daily, as opposed to the more common zero cleanings at home.

Even those who profess to actually clean their coffeemakers still can't overcome some of the disadvantages of home equipment, as Randall Buie of Henderson, Nevada, explains:

"It's not the coffee, it's the coffee*maker*. Commercial coffeemakers are made of stainless-steel brew baskets and copper or other metal water pipes. The average home coffeemaker is usually made with plastic brewing baskets and has rubber or rubberized tubing. Because coffee is made with heat, the hot water is much more susceptible to picking up odors and tastes in the brewing process than commercial units are."

Since we posed this Frustable, the infamous case in which McDonald's was sued for serving too-hot coffee (the plaintiff spilled coffee on her lap while carrying coffee in her automobile) occurred. McDonald's was attacked by her lawyers for brewing its coffee at unnecessarily high temperatures.

But contacts with folks in the coffee industry have revealed there is a good reason for this practice. Consumers prefer hot coffee. McDonald's' own market research revealed that consumers preferred *very* hot coffee to hot coffee, not just to keep it from cooling off prematurely but because it tastes better.

We spoke to Ingrid Anderson, of the redoubtable coffee chain Pasqua Inc., who told us that the optimum temperature for brewing coffee is approximately 195° Fahrenheit. Most home coffeemakers do not bring the water to this high a temperature. A significantly cooler brewing temperature risks extracting insufficient flavor from grounds; a higher temperature yields the "burnt" taste that typifies coffee put on too-hot burners in bad coffee shops. Most serious coffee emporiums wouldn't think of putting excess brewed coffee on burners, any more than a chef would keep an extra done steak on a hot broiler in case someone wanted to eat it hot. Starbucks, Pasqua, and other "gourmet" coffeehouses put extra brewed coffee in a vacuum, retaining the heat but not "overcooking" it.

Another constant refrain from commercial coffee purveyors we spoke to was that most home brewers do not put enough coffee into their coffeemakers to provide a rich cup of coffee. The recommended ratio, according to the experts we spoke to, should be two tablespoons of ground coffee per six ounces of water. Yet there is no uniformity among coffee measures handed out with coffee; nor is there even agreement about what constitutes a "cup" of water (it can range from five ounces to the expected eight ounces). Many home users mistakenly put in two tablespoons of coffee per eight ounces of water.

We heard from Carolyn Poulter, who runs a restaurant in Iowa and has a uniquely objective perspective—she lives above her own restaurant. She doesn't know if the commercial machine produces a hotter temperature for the water or if it provides a wider "spread" for the water when it falls on the grounds:

> "We have a domestic coffee machine in our apartment and you are right, it never tastes quite as good as running downstairs to the restaurant and using the [commercial] machine."

Even with all the advantages that institutional settings might provide, we were surprised that more of you didn't defend the quality of your own coffee. Even those of you who claimed that home coffee could be as flavorful as restaurant coffee offered other brewers as the hero. For example, Bill Gerk volunteers Kristin, an employee at a health store he frequents:

> "She has so much confidence that she wants to let you, me, or anyone else taste her coffee and compare with restaurant-brewed coffee. She seems certain that the preference will result in her coffee getting the prize over the restaurant-brewed coffee."

Gee, readers. We've been invited to a coffee taste test. Everyone off to Kristin's! We'll see if she has the proper grounds to stand on.

Original Imponderable submitted by Stuart Pomeranz of Stuart, Florida.

A complimentary book goes to Neil Parker of Summerland, British Columbia.

Frustable 10: Why Don't Women Spit More?

We thought this Frustable would generate more passion, but by and large we encountered a collective "Duh." Readers couldn't get past the knowledge gap created by the huge cultural divide between the sexes.

Many men were incredulous. Bob Kowalski of Detroit, Michigan, was typical of the male attitude:

> "Who says women don't spit more? They are probably just more discreet about it than the average male ('Hey, let's go for distance, guys!'). And those women who claim they never have such a need probably don't sweat, either. Ha!"

The only women we have ever seen spit were runners. So at least we know women are capable of spitting. But several females insisted that they don't feel the urge to expectorate. Well, not very often, anyway. Writes Debra Allen of Wichita Falls, Texas:

> "Why do men spit more? I don't know, but I do wish you'd stop. I can tell you, however, that we are not just repressing our own urge to expectorate. And when we do have to do it, we go off out of sight (and earshot) to do it. You're welcome."

Er, thank you.

When we were first researching this Frustable ourselves, the medical authorities we contacted indicated that there was no reason to believe that women didn't generate as much saliva as men. "Mr. Frustable," Bill Gerk, found a medical reference book that indicated that the average person manufactures two to three pints of saliva a day.

Most of you felt that socialization was the only possible answer. Lee Anne Hwang of Smyrna, Georgia, lobbies for this point of view:

> "It's that Western civilization princess-on-a-pedestal thing. A feminine flower would no more spit than she would sweat,

pee, snivel, or vomit. Such disgusting extrusions of body fluids were probably not even discussed in relation to women, once upon a time. Girls were probably cautioned to suppress as many eruptions of body fluids as they could possibly control. The urge to spit was probably bred out of the human female as a consequence.

Bill Gerk, although siding with the cultural socialization theory, picks up on Hwang's breeding hypothesis. He reminds us that Pavlov's experiments with dogs proved that conditioned reflexes can be used to inhibit as well as to induce salivation:

> "Salivary glands don't function mechanically, but are subject to the control of the brain. Salivary secretion is under the control of the nervous system and is stimulated reflexively by the sight, smell, and taste of food.
>
> "Could the social and psychological conditioning of the female actually reduce the amount of saliva produced in her mouth?"

We think the jury is still out on this subject. We didn't hear from any closeted female spitters, and assume there are some out there. Let's hear from you (we won't betray your nasty little secret).

Until then, we throw up our hands and wish we could embrace Lee Anne Hwang's alternate theory for why women don't spit more: "They're too busy shopping."

Original Imponderable submitted by Janet Wright of La Mesa, California. Thanks also to Melody Suppes of Palos Verdes, California; Joy Crist of Palmyra, New Jersey; Stephanie Papa of Baltimore, Maryland; and Marielle Marne of Fallston, Maryland.

A complimentary book goes to Lee Anne Hwang of Smyrna, Georgia.

The Frustables That Will Not Die

✎ If there's one thing we admire about *Imponderables'* readers, it's their tenacity. Long after we first try to quash a Frustable, readers are still offering new theories to solve the most perplexing mysteries that confront us. Herewith we present a status report on some Frustables that have bedeviled us in the past.

Please remember that we do not have space to review all the theories we advanced in the original write-ups; this section is meant as a supplement, not a replacement for the discussions in previous books.

✎ **Frustables First Posed in *Why Do Clocks Run Clockwise?* and First Discussed in *When Do Fish Sleep?***

Frustable 1: Why do you so often see one shoe lying on the side of the road?

Nearly ten years ago, when we posed the first Frustable, readers sent in *theories*. Now they send in confessions, leaving us with the unalterable impression that there's more than one way to create Single Shoe Syndrome ("SSS"). Listen to the inspiring tale of Marta Yaghnowvich of Oneonta, New York:

> "When my daughter was three years old, we went shoe shopping for her at a minimall with a long driveway and tall grass on each side. After we bought her new shoes, she wanted to wear them home, so I held the old pair in my hand, walked back to the car, let my daughter in the back seat, and threw the old shoes into the car without really paying attention to where they landed. (Hey, I was tired from shoe shopping with a three-year-old!)
>
> "I drove off, got home, noticed one old shoe missing, went back to the mall, searched the driveway, parking lot, and shoe store and finally found the old shoe in the tall grass by the side

of the road! If I didn't find it, someone else would have and probably written to you about it. And don't ask me why I was so persistent in finding an old shoe! I hate losing things."

Isn't this kind of persistence what made America great?

But when we think of persistence, we couldn't help marvel at the story of Donald E. Ullrich of Burlington, Iowa, who was a railway mail clerk back in the early 1950s. At that time, mail was often sorted in and delivered from moving trains. Ullrich worked the route between Chicago and Kansas City:

> "We didn't stop at every town, but while speeding along at sometimes 100 mph, a clerk assigned to 'local' duty would kick pouches of first class and sacks of newspapers (anything that would safely bounce) out the door at the station and also catch a pouch with mail from that town in a crane that was fastened on the mail car door. This took a certain amount of timing so that the clerk at the station didn't have to chase down a rolling pouch. A second or two of delay could force a trek of a mile or two to chase it.
>
> "One night, the 'local' clerk was in the process of changing from work clothes into dress clothes just prior to entering the KC yards when the last nonstop town came into view. He hadn't had time to tie his shoe strings and kicked the pouch, sacks, and one shoe out the door. In disgust, he took off the other shoe and threw it out the door, too.
>
> "The messenger waiting to pick up the mail noticed the flying first shoe and put it in the pouch to be picked up on the return trip that night. So he had to throw it away again.
>
> "That story's a recurring thought every time I see a single shoe on a roadway."

Poor Donald: Single Shoe Syndrome flashbacks!

We heard from Ariel Godwin, who lives in rural Earlville, New York. Amid a mundane report about finding a single man's shoe and a woman's sandal along the road, Godwin related a disturbing tale about hidden single-shoe repositories residing in the strangest places:

> "My aunt in Huntsville, Alabama, is familiar with a single shoe cemetery. When I was staying there in January 1993, we visited it. In the woods there's a huge pile of single shoes.
>
> "According to my aunt and uncle, the cemetery was there since they moved to Huntsville twenty years before. Although it has grown in the intervening years, they know not how.
>
> "A few months after my visit, my aunt sent us a package containing a shoe from the pile, and a letter instructing us to dump it in some obscure spot and thus plant the seed of a new single-shoe cemetery.
>
> "My aunt isn't a nut, she's just rather poetic. She enclosed a page of verse, a poem full of puns about 'soles' and 'souls.'
>
> "I therefore assert that SSS is not only upon us, but that there is no solution to it. What can we do?"

Move on to the next Frustable?

Frustable 3: Why do the British drive on the left and most other countries on the right?

Reader Theodore Mason of Carlsbad, California, conducted an impressive study of left-right variations in vehicles. His research confirmed most of what we said about the shift from left- to right-side-of-the-road driving in the U.S. Mason concurs with the original argument advanced by Richard Hopper (in *When Do Fish Sleep?*) that the American Conestoga wagon marked the turning point:

> "Most of the coaches, surreys, carriages, and wagons [before Conestoga wagons] had a place for the operator to sit on the right side next to a brake lever. The brake was operated by the driver's right hand or foot. There was also a receptacle on the right side of the vehicle designed to hold a whip when it was not being held by the driver . . ."

"So why do we drive on the right when we had been sitting on the right for so many years? I believe that when a driver approached oncoming traffic, the dirt, dust, rocks, water and mud that would fly up was avoided by driving on the right side of the road. The driver was exposed to the elements during the operation of the vehicle, but since he was sitting on the right side, he could avoid some of these problems by steering the horses in a direction that would offer some advantage. Of course, people sitting to the left of the driver would suffer all that the driver was avoiding, but the driver was in charge and most important in the operation of the vehicle."

Frustable 4: Why Is yawning contagious?

In *When Do Fish Sleep?*, we excitedly reported the news that psychologist Robert Provine has devoted much of his academic career to trying to solve this Frustable. Now he has competition. Reader Idria Barone of Ambler, Pennsylvania, thoughtfully sent us an October 29, 1994, article from *The Philadelphia Inquirer,* in which reporter Mark Bowden discusses the research of two psychologists, Rowan College professor Monica Greco and Temple University's Roy Benninger.

This duo has conducted many animal studies, and have made some bizarre observations, such as that giraffes don't yawn and predators yawn more than herbivores. Like Provine, Greco and Benninger confirm that yawning has nothing to do with oxygen deprivation. The psychologists believe that humans, like animals, yawn to keep themselves alert when falling asleep might be dangerous or inadvisable. While Provine theorizes that contagious yawning in humans might have been a method for primitive tribes to prepare for sleep, the Pennsylvania psychologists' animal studies lead them to an opposite conclusion:

"[Yawning] is a way for animals in a group to warn each other not to fall asleep. Behavior leaves no fossils, so there's no way to determine for certain how or why yawning is contagious. But there's a clue, Benninger says, in packs of chimpanzees who will take turns yawning in situations where nothing much is going on, but where it is not safe to fall asleep."

☞ **Frustables First Posed in** *Why Do Dogs Have Wet Noses?* **and First Answered in** *Do Penguins Have Knees?*

Frustable 3: We often hear the cliché "We only use 10 percent of our brains." How was it determined that we use 10 percent and not 5 percent or 15 percent?

We think that reader Wesley McDermott finally found the citation we have been seeking in Robert Heinlein's work that pertains to this Frustable. It can be found in "Gulf," a short story in the collection *Assignment in Eternity:*

> "Around World War II Dr. Samuel Renshaw at the Ohio State University was proving that most people are about one-fifth efficient in using their capacities to see, hear, taste, feel, and remember. His research was swallowed in the morass of communist pseudoscience that obtained after World War III . . ."

McDermott agrees with our conclusion that the 10 percent figure more likely stemmed from the writings of Dale Carnegie, especially because at least where he comes from, one-fifth does not equal 10 percent.

Frustable 4: Where, exactly, did the expression "Blue Plate Special" come from?

While reading Joan and Lydia Wilen's *More Chicken Soup and Other Folk Remedies,* reader Tanya Ninaus uncovered a startling theory for why blue plate specials were blue instead of, say, ecru. The authors cite color therapist Carlton Wagner, who claims that blue food is unappetizing and that restaurants know about this response. There-fore, restaurants served food on blue plates so that they'd save money on all-you-can-eat specials. We don't buy this explanation for a second, but it *is* ingenious.

Frustable 6: Why do dogs tilt their heads when you talk to them?

We've already fielded arguments among readers who believe that the tilt is primarily a function of hearing, and those who think it has more to do with vision. Jim Kazek of Madison, Alabama, who has owned German shepherds for more than thirty years, thinks the so-lution is a combination of the two. He conducted many experi-ments with his current shepherd, and came to these conclusions:

1. Dogs don't always tilt their heads when you speak to them.
2. They tilt more when you are four or more feet away—there-fore, their limited visual acumen must have something to do with their actions.
3. The angle of vision was relevant. The tilting occurred only when Jim was above the dog.
4. Despite a limited vocabulary, dogs react to differing speech patterns:

> "A nearly 100 percent success rate for induced head tilting can be attributed to the interrogative form of speech. When we ask a question, we tend to lift the end of the sentence so that the object of our conversation is aware that we are, indeed, asking a question. Dogs are tilting their heads *the same way humans do* when confronted with a pitch above what can be considered 'normal' range."

Frustable 9: Why does the heart depicted in illustrations look totally different than a real heart?

We've already advanced theories that the idealized heart represents everything from human buttocks and testicles to frogs' hearts. So can we be shocked that reader John Boose of Seattle, Washington, learned in elementary school that the stylized heart depicts two affectionate swan necks and heads?

> "Swans supposedly mate for life and spend much time together as adults. The facing swan heads thus became a romantic symbol and were associated with the human heart, our traditional seat of romantic attachment."

Frustable 10: Where do all the missing pens go?

We thought we'd heard it all. We are humbled by this contribution from Elizabeth Garrott of Louisville, Kentucky:

> "I know where my latest lost pen went. I had just pulled the lever behind the commode at work, when the pen fell out of my pocket and into the whirlpool. Will the pen turn up somewhere down the Ohio [River]?"

❧ **Frustables First Posed in** *Do Penguins Have Knees?* **and First Answered in** *When Did Wild Poodles Roam the Earth?*

Frustable 1: Why do doctors have such bad penmanship?

We heard from a professional graphologist whose father was a physician for more than forty years. Andrea McNichol, director of Graphology Consultants International, offers three theories to explain this Frustable, all advanced by readers in the past:

1. Doctors are in a hurry most of the time, leading to sloppy and rushed writing.
2. Doctors are under heavy pressure at work, leading to "stressed," uneven, and poorly formed penmanship.
3. They write illegibly on purpose.

We were particularly interested in amplification of McNichol's third argument, which has been alluded to by readers in the past. McNichol claims that some doctors write illegibly in order to cover their tracks in case they are accused of malpractice:

> "Should there be trouble later on, the doctors are covered because they can claim they wrote whatever they want people to think they wrote. I think this reason #3 is applicable in only about 10 percent of the cases [of bad penmanship], however.
>
> "I do work on many 'doctored doctor records' cases, and unfortunately, there are a small number of doctors who are intentionally illegible in what they write about their patients."

Frustable 2: Why are salt and pepper the standard condiments on home and restaurant tables?

Neil B. Schanker, assistant professor of biology at William Rainey Harper College, adds another argument for salt's omnipresence on tables:

"While many spices have pleasing tastes, salt is essential for life. The human nervous system requires potassium and sodium. A vegetable diet provides plenty of potassium but no sodium. Since we must have sodium in our diet, it makes sense to have salt (sodium chloride) as a standard condiment."

Frustable 8: How was hail measured before golf balls were invented?

Reader Maxey Brooke of Dallas, Texas, was kind enough to pass along a feature from the *Dallas Morning News* that quoted the National Weather Service's list of objects used as metaphors for different hail sizes. We are dubious about how often they are used in practice by meteorologists and even more incredulous about the accuracy of some of the measurements (these figures seem to refer to diameters rather than circumferences):

Pea—$\frac{1}{4}$ inch
Marble—$\frac{1}{2}$ inch
Penny or dime—$\frac{3}{4}$ inch
Nickel or quarter—1 inch
Susan B. Anthony dollar or Kennedy half-dollar—$1\frac{1}{4}$ inches
Walnut—$1\frac{1}{2}$ inches
Golf ball—$1\frac{3}{4}$ inches
Hen egg—2 inches
Tennis ball—$2\frac{1}{2}$ inches
Baseball—$2\frac{3}{4}$ inches
Teacup—3 inches
Grapefruit—4 inches
Softball—$4\frac{1}{2}$ inches

When was the last time you saw a weather forecast refer to "Susan B. Anthony dollar-sized hail"? Mother Nature must have a bias toward $1\frac{3}{4}$-inch hail.

David Feldman

❦ Frustables First Posed in *When Did Wild Poodles Roam the Earth?* and First Answered in *How Does Aspirin Find a Headache?*

Frustable 1: Why do women often go to the rest room together? And what are they doing in there for so long?

After our comprehensive discussion of this topic in *How Does Aspirin Find a Headache?*, we figured no new theories would be advanced. But, alas, this topic is still on the cusp of popular consciousness. Indeed, on a recent episode of *Hangin' With Mr. Cooper*, Mr. C. asked two teenage girls why they spent a half hour in the bathroom. One responded, "At least we wash our hands."

Laura Caples, the only *Imponderables* contributor we know of who lives in a town named after the lead singer of U2 and a U.S. congressman (Bono, Arkansas), added three new alternatives to our mix:

> "1. The women don't know where the rest room is and they hope the other women do.
> "2. They don't want to be talked about if they do not go to the rest room with other women.
> "3. They want to talk about the women that did not come to the rest room."

In our original discussion of this Frustable, we included a comparative flow chart contrasting the nineteen steps taken by the typical woman versus the eight by men. To refresh your memory, here was our description of the typical man's trip to a public rest room:

Open door or enter doorway
Step to urinal
Unzip
Do business
Flush (optional)
Wash hands (optional)
Dry hands (conceivable)
Leave

Reader Martin Nakashian of Everett, Massachusetts, indicates that perhaps we should have added a ninth step: "You forgot to zip up!" So *that's* why we have been getting those stares. We thought it was our boyish good looks.

Frustable 4: Women generally possess more body fat than men. So why do women tend to feel colder than men in the same environment?

Two more theories to add to the mix. One comes from Barbara Smith of Montpelier, Vermont:

> "It's true that men usually do have more muscle mass than women. Muscles burn many more calories than fat and therefore produce more heat when you compare the BMR (basal metabolic rate) of men and women—men are usually higher due to their increased muscle mass. The higher BMR tells us the rate at which we burn calories.
>
> "So men have more muscle mass and a higher BMR, which tells us they are burning more calories. Therefore, they are producing more heat and feel warmer.
>
> "Pregnant women and babies also have a higher BMR and are usually warmer than other women."

Biologist Neil Schanker's theory:

> "Sensations of being hot or cold are contained in the skin. Due to estrogen, females have more subcutaneous (under-the-skin) fat.
>
> "More subcutaneous fat makes it more difficult for one's internal heat to get to the skin. Result: At least in my experience, women want to turn up the thermostat or wear more sweaters than men."

Frustable 5: Why is the average woman a much better dancer than the average man?

We were intrigued and impressed with this theory advanced by Lee Anne Hwang of Smyrna, Georgia:

> "Men just can't seem to get that hip action.
>
> "It's true. On the whole, men seem to be better dancers in other cultures than in the good ol' U.S. of A. And I think it's because to be a really good dancer, you have to get that pelvis grinding. If you can loosen your hips, the whole body loosens up and becomes more fluid. For women, swaying of the hips is practiced from girlhood, because such motions were considered sexy in women. . . . Obviously, since the motion is so strongly associated with feminine sex appeal, men don't learn it and are embarrassed to display any motion they think resembles it. They all *can*—ask a man to imitate the way he thinks a woman walks—they just don't.
>
> "In support of this theory, just turn on some Barney songs and watch a room full of four-year-olds dance. The girls and boys dance pretty much the same. The difference comes later when they begin to learn the body language of their respective genders."

Of course, Hwang's theory doesn't explain why women fox-trot better than men, but I think we'll let it rest.

Speaking of rest, we admire the moxie of Kate Flack of Bexley, Ohio, who attempts to kill two Frustables with one stone:

> "At my first junior high school dance, I was miserable because, like many other girls, I did not know how to dance. Instead, I leaned against a wall with some of my friends, watching some of the other girls who seemed to have some idea of what they were doing.
>
> "After a while, one of my friends left to go to the bathroom. Ten minutes later, she still hadn't returned, and the rest of us went to look for her. I really can't tell you why all of us

went together to look for her—maybe we were afraid that the Swamp Thing had gotten her and didn't want her to face it alone.

"The moment we entered the bathroom, we saw why she had been in there for such a long time. There was our friend, standing with many of the other good-dancer-wanna-be's, taking lessons from one of the few true Good Dancers. Needless to say, my friends and I immediately forgot all about leaving— we stayed and learned along with everyone else."

So *that's* what women are doing for so long in the rest room together. We can report with a clear conscience that we have never seen a conga line forming in a men's rest room.

Frustable 7: Why do very few restaurants serve celery with mixed green salads?

Reader Angela Stockton of Gulfport, Mississippi, writes:

> "I'm surprised no one mentioned that celery contains a lot of water. If I have leftover salad, I don't bother to save it for another day. The water in the celery will seep out and turn all the other crisp vegetables unappetizingly soggy."

To bolster her argument, Angela then answers an unasked Imponderable: Why don't you see celery in avian salad bars?

> "When my daughter acquired her pet bird, the veterinarian reminded us to feed it not just seeds, but also fruits and vegetables. But celery was a specific no-no; the vet explained that because it is so watery, it gives birds diarrhea."

Frustable 8: In English spelling, why does "i" come before "e" except after "c"?

In *How Does Aspirin Find a Headache?*, we whined about a lack of response to this Frustable. When we originally posed this question, we mused: "We wonder where this arcane rule came from?" Many of you wanted to share all the exceptions to the rule, which was exactly the point of the question: What good is this "rule" when it is violated so often?

The putative mnemonic for the spelling rule is:

> "Put 'i' before 'e'
> Except after 'c,'
> Or when sounded like 'a'
> As in neighbor and weigh;
> And except seize and seizure
> And also leisure,
> Weird, height, and either,
> Forfeit and neither."

But these exceptions are far from definitive. Several readers sent us a citation from William Safire's 1990 book *Fumblerules,* in which the author humorously scoffs at the power of mnemonic devices to exhaust the complications of "i before e":

> "Only the other day I had occasion to shout, 'Seize the sheik, friend, before he does further mischief!' That's one way to keep track of the damned exceptions.
> "As Karl Marx never wrote: 'Spellers of the world, untie.' "

We can quantify the degree of exceptions to the rule thanks to the painstaking research of Larry J. Van Stone of Stillwater, Oklahoma, who analyzed the contents of a computerized spelling dictionary that contains approximately 100,000 words—not the entire English language, to be sure, but a weighty, representative sample. Here is what Van Stone's research revealed:

621 WORDS FOLLOW THE RULE (OR SEEM TO)

In 381 words, the diphthong "ie" is used in a variety of ways: (e.g., befriend, diesel, fief, Poughkeepsie).

In 154 words, "ie" is not a diphthong but a syllable division: (e.g. anxiety, diet, siesta).

In 24 words, "ei" follows "c" as the rule states: (e.g., deceit; ceiling; receive).

In one word, "ei" is used as a syllable division, though the "e" is a French accented vowel (i.e., glacéing).

In 61 words, including 18 "weigh" words, "ei" sounds like a long "a" (e.g., lightweight, freight, Beirut).

372 WORDS BREAK THE RULE (OR SEEM TO)

In 77 words, "ie" follows "c" because the word is the plural of a noun that ends in "cy" (e.g., autocracies, intricacies, bankruptcies).

In one word, "ie" follows "c" because it is derived from a verb that ends in "cy" (i.e., fancied).

9 pairs of words are the comparative and superlative forms of adjectives that end in "cy" (e.g., chancier and chanciest, racier and raciest).

3 names contain "cie" as all or part of a single syllable (i.e., Francie, Gracie, Mercier)

In 2 words, "ie" is a syllable division (i.e., hacienda and society).

27 words contain "ie" after "c" because of Latin origins:

9 contain the string "cient"; in all but "ancient," the longer string "ficient" or "facient" comes from the Latin for "make" (e.g., ancient, sufficient).

10 contain the string "scien" from "know" in Latin (e.g., conscience, science).

3 contain "species" and its relatives (i.e., species, subspecies, interspecies).

5 others are miscellaneous exceptions: (e.g., glacier, concierge); 94 words have "ei" not following "c," pronounced various ways:

In 21 words, "ei" sounds like a long "e" (e.g., caffeine, seize, Keith)

In 6 words, "ei" sounds like a short "e" (e.g., heifer, their, peignoir)

In 57 words, "ei" sounds like a long "i," including 8 "stein's" (e.g., Liechtenstein, seismology, Heinz)

In 5 words, "ei" sounds like a short "i" (e.g., forfeit, weird)

Ɗavid Ƒeldman

In 5 words, "ei" is a schwa (unstressed vowel sound) (e.g., foreign, sovereign)

In 149 words, "ei" is not pronounced "a" and is not a diphthong, but is a syllable division (e.g., nucleic, deism, reinstitute).

Van Stone's statistical summary of percentages of compliance with the so-called "rule":

Of 669 words containing "ie," 128 have it following "c" and 541 do not, for 81 percent compliance with the law (including the exception of "preceded by c").

Of 329 words containing "ei," 61 sound like a long "a," 25 precede it with "c," while 243 contain "ei" sounded in other ways and not preceded by "c," for only 26 percent compliance with the exceptions.

So, of the 993 words analyzed, 54 percent comply with the main rule; 9 percent comply with one of the exceptions; and 37 percent do not comply. And we wonder why non-natives have problems spelling in English!

So how have we gotten into this sad situation, where spelling of individual words must come from rote memory rather than logical deduction? There seem to be two main causes. The first has been the tendency of what reader Bill Gerk thinks is an expression that soon will be on all of our lips: "Orthography recapitulates Ortheopy." We love you, Bill, but we don't think this is going to replace "Where's the beef?" as a great American catchphrase.

Luckily, Bill supplies a translation of his catchphrase: "Proper spelling reflects pronunciation." Bill supplied two citations to support his theory. One is from John B. Opdycke's *Say What You Mean* (Funk and Wagnalls, 1944):

"English spelling has always been more considerate of the ear than of the eye, chiefly because the tongue has forced it to be. In other words, the human tongue is so intolerant of sound and fury signifying nothing that, regardless of word derivation, it sometimes 'lops off' letters that do not please it—refuses to be unduly twisted by clumsy letter combinations and awkward syllabification."

Spelling and even pronunciation were far from stable. Only the advent of dictionaries and the spread of printing on a mass scale helped change the equation, as Bill Bryson describes in his book *The Mother Tongue* (Morrow: 1990):

". . . the trend was clearly towards standardization, which was effectively achieved by about 1650.

"Unluckily for us, English spellings were becoming fixed at the time when the language was undergoing one of those great phonetic seizures that periodically unsettle any tongue. The result is that we have today in English a body of spellings that, for the most part, faithfully reflect the pronunciations of people living 400 years ago."

If the tendency of English spelling to mimic pronunciation leads to many exceptions, so does a second cause: the intermixing of languages in Europe. Van Stone noted that most of the words that follow the "i before e" rule have Latin roots and that many of the exceptions are Germanic in origin. And these exceptions date back to eruptions in Europe nearly 1,000 years ago. The Normans, who occupied Normandy in the tenth century and conquered England in the next, had a profound influence on the English language and its spelling, as reader Neil Parker explains:

"Enter the Normans, with their Frank way of speaking. Now English is enriched, not only by new words, but by the new pronunciations that accompany them. Words that began originally as Latin, like 'conceive' (French: *concevoir*), 'perceive' (French: *percevoir*), 'receive' (French: *recevoir*). English pronunciation tends to accent the last syllable of these words and therefore to lengthen it to the long 'e' sound. But the spelling retains its roots by keeping the 'e' next to the 'c'—as it was in the original."

Anything we can do about making sense of all these conflicting currents in English spelling? Nope, concludes Van Stone, and partly because our language always evolves:

> "The grammatical rules we were taught are mostly out of date. The word 'grammar' originated as a synonym for 'Latin,' being the Latin word for 'literature.' Grammar schools were originally (in the sixteenth century) places children were taught enough Latin to read the Classics, from which their liberal education was expected to derive. Secondary schools added fluency in Latin so scholars could converse regardless of their mother tongue, and enforced thousands of hours of compulsory reading and recitation that prepared the mind for a lifetime of study. Education was the responsibility of the individual, once this preparative foundation was laid.
>
> "Today's grammatical rules only truly apply to that part of the English language (one-third, and dropping fast) that derives from Latin and the Romance languages. Even this much Latin in our Germanic tongue derives primarily from a few centuries of Norman occupation of England after 1066."

A complimentary book goes to Larry J. Van Stone of Stillwater, Oklahoma.

Frustable 9: What in the world are grocery store managers looking for when they approve personal checks?

If we may get back to earth after our learned discussion of orthography, we're proud to say that nobody had any major beefs with our discussion of store managers and their bizarre check-approval policies. But one of our most prolific correspondents, reader Erik Reichmann, who now works at a nongrocery retail store, thinks that we got the "trees" right but missed the "forest":

> "I'm surprised nobody mentioned what I think is a likely reason for the rigmarole surrounding checks: The stores want to discourage customers from writing them. And with good rea-

son, because checks are the riskiest form of payment. With a credit card, a computer hookup can tell you within seconds whether the customer has sufficient credit on her account; but even if the computer could disclose a customer's checking account balance (and I'm sure it can), it would only reveal what the balance is at that moment, not whether there are any checks outstanding that might clear before the store deposits this one.

"I personally wish my store didn't accept checks, because they're a royal pain to process. When I was training on the register, it took me a whole day to learn the twelve things to look for in accepting checks, not to mention the procedure for ringing them through. Plus we have to check each account in a little file box that contains the names of all the creeps who've bounced checks in our store in the past. . . . The only reason stores continue to accept checks is that if they didn't, they would stand to lose some substantial sales from customers who have no other means of paying."

At least it's nice to know that the managers as well as us customers are being tortured by check-approval policies.

Frustable 10: Why do so many policemen wear mustaches?

In *How Does Aspirin Find a Headache?*, we chronicled the many police officers who wrote to us explaining that mustaches made them look less "soft" and more macho. The ever-erudite Bill Gerk found a citation in R. Dale Guthrie's *Body Hot Spots* (Van Nostrand Reinhold: 1976) that offers a tantalizing theory that might be a motivation for some police officers to put some fur on their upper lips:

". . . in order to promote the dominant image one must not reveal the weak, whining lip of the subordinate. One way is to reduce all emotion—to keep a straight face, a stiff upper lip.

"Moustaches—that is, the untrimmed variety—fan sideways and down over the upper lip, blotting out virtually all visual communication by the mouth. They fan out around the edges of the mouth, hiding or at least buffering the signal value of cheek wrinkles and the position of the mouth's corner . . . The constant 'flat' signal transmission in the face of fear, anxiety, tension, or pain promotes an unswerving, persevering, secure image—the image of a high dominant, someone on top of it all."

Letters

✌ *We can't satisfy everyone. Indeed, sometimes it seems we can't satisfy* anyone. *That's why we've always reserved the Letters section not for the introduction of new Imponderables or Frustables theories, or even letters of praise, as much as we are tempted to include them. This space is reserved for those of you who have bones to pick with us. And there are many, many bones in the human body.*

We receive thousands of letters every year, and can publish only a fraction of the many more that deserve airing. Many of you have proposed corrections or suggestions that we will try to verify; it can take years sometimes, but corrections have been made in later printings of earlier books thanks to your efforts.

But enough stalling. Time for you to have your shot at us.

Could book titles have an impact upon the mood of a readership? Letters published in How Does Aspirin Find a Headache? *seemed to indicate that more than a few of you were in a testy mood: a collective migraine, perhaps? We're happy to say that you are a kinder, gentler lot for* Hyenas.

For some reason, many of you obsessed about matters geographical this time around. We heard from Dale Kapperich of Kent, Washington:

"I've noticed a lot of entries in your book come from Washington State. Does this mean we are highly intelligent? Or the opposite?"

There is no such thing as a dumb question. So that must mean Washingtonians are a smart group, right? Or else you are drinking too many lattes up there in the Northwest.

But some of you don't share our enthusiasm for the good citizens of Washington, namely Alan J. Gryfe of Buffalo, New York, who disputes the account of the origins of Boeing's 707 model number as described by the largest employer in Seattle (first discussed in Why Do Dogs Have Wet Noses?*):*

"I wish to dispute your explanation of Boeing's model 707. Frankly, if you believe the explanation that Boeing's P.R. hacks give you, you're letting them pound sand up your *tochus*.

"As detailed by no less an authority than the Smithsonian's National Air & Space Museum in Washington D.C., the original 707 was built as the prototype Boeing model 367-80 and assigned the registration number N70700. Boeing employees started referring to the new plane as '707' and the nickname stuck so strongly that Boeing eventually bowed to the inevitable and continued numbering its jet models in the 7X7 series. . . ."

Readers' geographical concerns were bicoastal, though. Sheri Radford of Victoria, British Columbia, wanted to muse further about our discussion of "New York Steaks" in How Does Aspirin Find a Headache?:

"You can't find 'New York Steaks' in New York for the same reason that French people don't 'French kiss'—names of faraway places are more alluring. Years ago I met a French guy, and he said that particular type of kissing is called 'English kissing' by the French."

Those that can't cook, kiss, we guess.

We are relieved that the battle between geographers and biologists over the difference between a pond and a lake seems to have subsided. But Steven Kozak of Huntington, New York, writes to inform us that geologists might dispute our geographically oriented answer to what differentiates a mountain from a hill in When Do Fish Sleep?:

"The geologic meaning of a mountain is an area of relief that has 'zonal vegetations': at different elevations, different kinds of plants or trees can survive. Therefore, the Catskill 'Mountains' are really just hills, because they are covered by the same type of vegetation. . . ."

In our first book, Imponderables, *we tackled the mystery of why some houses have addresses ending in "halves." Brad Johnson of Boston, Massachusetts, adds another reason we had never heard before:*

> "My house was built in 1864 by Victorians. Being superstitious, they did not want to use the number 13. Instead, the numbers on my side of the street are numbered 11, 11½, 15."

But we contemporary folk reject superstition. In every book since the original discussion of why ranchers hang boots upside down on fenceposts in Why Do Clocks Run Clockwise?, *our letters section has contained further theories or sightings. Cynthia Ducksworth of Mayo, Florida, continues the tradition, offering a totally practical explanation for the ritual:*

> "When a pair of leather boots gets wet and you leave them lying around, it is almost impossible to get them back on again. So we always placed them on fenceposts or something similar (now there are boot trees) so that the neck would dry straight, making them easier to get on."

But might all those ranchers have dogs? Retrievers, in particular? Robert F. Arnesen of Tucson, Arizona, sent us an Associated Press photograph of a dog looking up longingly at a boot and a shoe suspended from a tree. The caption reads:

> "Molson, whose owner is Cyndi Driem of Green Oak Township, Mich., is shown with two of the many shoes she has collected from neighborhood homes. Driem puts the items on a tree near the road so her neighbors can pick up any belongings Molson might have taken from them."

Unfortunately, the caption does not reveal if Driem had fence posts available as an alternative to the tree.

Speaking of Molson, readers had other beverages on their mind. Steve Thompson of La Crescenta, California, adds to our discussion of Dr Pepper, and in particular, why there is no period after the "r" in "Dr":

"In 1963, Dr Pepper adopted a new lettering style; the letter "r" consisted of a straight line and a dot to the upper-right of it. The company was forced to delete the period because then the letter would have looked like an "i" followed by a colon. In subsequent lettering styles, the period was never restored."

Speaking of beverages, how about water? We can't live without it. In When Did Wild Poodles Roam the Earth?, *we mused about why, in old movies and television shows, when women were about to give birth at home, someone, usually the hapless husband, was dispatched hurriedly to boil water. Emily Harris, a certified nursing assistant from Davenport, Iowa, thought our discussion of hot water was full of hot air:*

"No, it wasn't to sterilize things. Not to keep husbands and kids busy. Not to make tea for the doctor or midwife.

"Hot salt water, and lots of it, was applied to the vaginal opening to facilitate stretching. The old midwives didn't make use of incisions and stitches used today. That's why you didn't see what was done with the hot water—they couldn't show that in a movie."

They did let the water cool down a little, *didn't they?*

As long as we're in a squeamish mood, let's cite the contribution of Donna D. Phillips of Catlin, Illinois, to our discussion of why starving people often have bloated stomachs, first discussed in How Does Aspirin Find a Headache?:

"All of your answers are true, but in some areas of much starvation, especially in Africa, the parasite levels are high. Many people are infected with bilharzia [also known as 'schistosomiasis,' a disease in which parasites live in the blood vessels], which also causes major stomach bloating, no matter how much food one ingests. Some of the 'starving people' pictures depict people suffering from this disease."

David Feldman

While we are discussing grim subjects, Joseph Lee Schiff of Syracuse, New York, was not at all happy with our discussion of "Why do we bury the dead with their heads toward the west facing east?" in Aspirin:

> "Judaism traces its root back over 5,755 years ago, and Jews all over the world were, from the beginning of time, and are to this very day, buried facing east. . . .
>
> ". . . We are all—all religions—buried facing east so as to face the Holy Land. Even the Pharaohs were thus buried."

While it's not true that all religions are buried with the same orientation, or recognize the same Holy Land, for that matter, we should have made it clear that we were referring to Christian burials.

If we may proceed to more pleasant medical musings, at the end of our discussion of why dogs wiggle their rear legs when scratched on the belly or chest (in When Did Wild Poodles Roam the Earth?*), we concluded with a throwaway line, "We'd like to think that our human knee-jerk reflex might also have a purpose . . ." Dr. Richard E. Barlow of Dunwoody, Georgia, was kind enough to supply an explanation for why this procedure serves some purpose other than being the only medical test that we actually enjoy:*

> "You may be surprised that the knee jerk is quite important to us. This is a deep tendon stretch reflex activated through the spinal cord. The 'reflex' ensures that the motion occurs even before the sensory input of the tendon stretch reaches the brain. When the patellar tendon is stretched with the knees crossed, the result is the somewhat ridiculous response where the leg kicks out wildly, often endangering the person who tapped the knee.
>
> "When the tendon stretch occurs as a result of taking a step, however, the response is quite necessary. The antigravity muscles of the thigh are almost immediately tensed, thus supporting the body weight and preventing the knee from buckling under us. Indeed, loss of the knee-jerk reflex may result in a difficult gait disorder.
>
> "We also have tendon stretch reflexes at the heel and in the upper extremities. The arm reflexes are generally less vio-

lent and do represent a more vestigial reflex from our days on all fours, evolutionarily speaking. These reflexes, however, still are important to us. Think of the automatic tensing of the arm muscles that occurs when a heavy load is placed in your arms. Without the reflex, the load would likely wind up on the floor."

While we are on the subject of being on all fours on the floor, we can't help but think of our friend, the cockroach. And it's particularly comforting to think of dead roaches. We heard from David Sheppard of Wichita, Kansas, who not only works for the largest pest-control company in the world but also raises cockroaches as a hobby (sic). Dave takes issue with some of the entomologists we cited in When Do Fish Sleep?, *who tried to explain why roaches die on their backs:*

"The simple answer is that roaches don't always die on their backs. Most of the roaches people see dead are exposed to pesticides. The most common pesticides today have active ingredients that are cholinesterase inhibitors. Cholinesterase is the enzyme that allows muscles to relax. The inhibition of this enzyme causes the muscles to contract uncontrollably. The dead roaches that most people see died from massive convulsions. These convulsions are what caused them to fall onto their backs.

"Those that die naturally tend to die in an entirely natural position. They tend to look like they are just standing there. Specialized pads on their feet allow them to grip a surface, so when not affected by pesticides, they tend to die standing up."

Luckily, in the two years since the publication of How Does Aspirin Find a Headache?, *we received only one letter like this (from Audrey Stehr of Palm Beach Gardens, Florida) in response to the Imponderable "Why don't we ever see cockroaches in our usually crumb-filled car?":*

"When I first moved to South Florida in 1982, my husband and I bought a used car. Later that evening, after it got dark, and we opened the car door and the interior light came on, at least 100 roaches of all sizes scattered.

"Let me tell you, the drive home that night was pure torture. It took a few weeks, a few boxes of roach pills, a few roach motels, and a can of Raid to get rid of those roaches. And a few months later, I still had a roach appear on the door frame as I was driving down I-95 at 65 mph. It's a good thing traffic was light."

Audrey, if other drivers knew what you were experiencing, you would have seen cars scampering away from you faster than any roaches.

While we're discussing scampering away on the highway, our man in Bloomington, Illinois, Paul "Funn" Dunn, passed along a follow-up to an Imponderable from our first book, in which we described why traffic jams seem to occur (and then dissipate) for no discernible reason. In the August 1, 1994, Newsweek article "Why Does Traffic Jam?," reporter Sharon Begley chronicles the research of University of California, Berkeley, researcher Michael Cassidy, who studies traffic patterns as 'wave motions over time and space.' Cassidy's research corroborates our depiction of many traffic jams as being caused by irrational driving. In particular, he observes that drivers 'lose their manhood' if they allow another car to slip in front of them on a highway. When they see an influx of traffic approaching (from an on-ramp, for example), they speed up prematurely and then slow down once they see that mergers aren't a threat:

"This deceleration starts perhaps a mile past the merge point, quite the opposite of traffic experts' assumption that the effect of merges is felt in back of them. If Cassidy is right, traffic flow can be understood as a unique combination of wave mechanics . . . and testosterone poisoning."

Or perhaps cockroach avoidance.

It's a good thing we don't have more graffiti inside tunnels. That might cause a traffic jam, too. But reader Matt Conrad of Bloomington, Indiana, points out that in Poodles, *we neglected to mention one advantage of lining ceramic tiles on the interior of tunnels:*

"Most cities have a problem with spray-painted graffiti. Paint comes off ceramic easily with scouring powder, or probably even with high-pressure water sprayers. Removing paint from concrete must be done with sandblasting or acid, both of which will leave a patch of concrete lighter than the surrounding area. Removing paint from ceramic leaves no such evidence behind."

While we are still on the road, as it were, we have another addendum from Allen C. Demmin of Middleton, Wisconsin, to supplement our answer to David Letterman's Imponderable about why auto manufacturers have moved the brights/dimmer switch from the floorboard to the stalk of the steering column (discussed in Aspirin*):*

"Our son has an artificial right leg, due to a birth defect. When he was ready to take driver education, a few years ago, we had to equip our car with a left-foot accelerator. Along with this piece of equipment came a warning that a steering post dimmer must accompany this attachment. This was obvious, for a left-footed driver must use the foot for both the foot-feed and the brake pedal, and cannot use a floor dimmer switch."

And in our last road-related letter, Julian Shaw takes us to task for two words we wrote in How Does Aspirin Find a Headache? *'s discussion of how engineers decide where to put curves on highways. The two words that incurred Shaw's wrath: "lay cement."*

"Cement is expensive if you are trying to cover a road, say six inches deep, and a mile long. Cement, as its name implies, is a cementing agent, a locking-together binder. To keep costs in line, we mix cement, water, sand, and typically, crushed stone to get 'concrete.' So it is this 'concrete' that we lay."

We'll change our wording for future editions. We hope all is forgiven.
We don't usually include discussions of Who Put the Butter in Butterfly? *(our book about English word origins) here, but we thought that Dr. John Parr's (of Coarsegold, California) note would be of general interest. We*

claimed that the "she" in the expression "That's all she wrote" probably re-
ferred to the "Everywoman" who wrote the infamous "Dear John" letters to
soldiers during World War II. Parr remembers a music-hall song that his
mother sang (not in a music hall, but in the kitchen while cooking). The
lyrics he remembers are:

> "There was I, waiting at the church,
> She left me in the lurch,
> Oh, how she did upset me!
> She left me a note, this is all she wrote,
> 'I can't get away to marry you today—
> My wife won't let me.' "

In his book You Could Look It Up, *William Safire published a letter from*
a reader with a longer version of the same lyric. We don't have any explana-
tion for the change in gender (which raises our suspicions) or any solid proof
that the expression stems from this song, but it certainly is plausible.

While we are delving into the issue of gender confusion, Sheri Radford is
back with a startling confession that relates to our discussion in Aspirin
about why Barbie has realistic nylon hair while Ken is stuck with plastic or
painted hair:

"When I was a little girl who played with Barbies, way back in
the early 1980s, I had a Ken doll with hair. The hair was so
short, though, that it very quickly stuck out in all directions
and looked really ugly. Barbie's hair was so long that it could
be brushed and put in a ponytail, but poor Ken was stuck with
a perpetual bad hair day. Needless to say, I didn't like this Ken
much and soon replaced him with one with plastic hair.

"I disagree with those who say that Ken isn't important,
though. My friends and I needed a Ken, so that Barbie would
have someone to kiss (and later to do other things with . . .).
My friend Nancy didn't have a Ken doll, so she took one of her
Barbies and cut off all its hair, and then made the proper male
appendage (you know what I mean) out of masking tape and
added it to the doll."

No, Sheri. We have absolutely no idea what you mean.

Moving right along, Steve Thompson claims that we were confused when we referred to agent Jim Trupin as our Boswell, "Tom Boswell." When we later referred to his wife as our Marion Ross, Steve wondered whether we were thinking of biographer James Boswell or Happy Days' *Tom Bosley. Let's put it this way, Steve. We don't see ourselves as Samuel Johnson. Oops. We attribute 15 percent of this mistake to our agent.*

Speaking of mistakes, many of us make them on the first Tuesday after the first Monday in November every four years or so. In Poodles, *we discussed why federal elections weren't just held on, say, the first or second Tuesday of the month. J. Bradley King, a lawyer in Indianapolis, Indiana, provides a compelling addition to our discussion, including original source material to back up his contentions:*

"The answer lies in a basic election law principle: since election laws are chock-full of deadlines (for filing to be a candidate, for registering to vote, or to file a petition for a recount), if the legislature changes (or creates) a date in election law, it must be prepared to also change other election dates."

King explains that a uniform election day bill was proposed by Representative Alexander Duncan, a Whig from Ohio, who noted that

". . . an existing federal election law required the presidential electors to meet on the first Wednesday in December *and within thirty-four days after they were chosen by the voters.* Since more than thirty-four days could pass between an election on the first Tuesday in November (which could occur as early as November 1) and the meeting of the presidential electors on the first Wednesday in December (which would occur as late as December 7), Congress had a choice: It could either move the November election date set in the bill or change the December date for the presidential elector meeting.

"It chose to leave the existing law on presidential electors alone, and went with the 'first Tuesday after the first Monday' date for the new law on presidential elections. In later years, when other federal and state election dates were made uniform, legislatures simply followed the 1845 'first Tuesday after first Monday' formula.

"The irony, though, is that Congressman Duncan's solution didn't quite solve the problem: there are in fact 35 days between the first possible date for a presidential election (November 2) and the last possible date for a first Wednesday in December (December 7). The dilemma has finally been solved by doing what Rep. Duncan wished to avoid in 1845: the 'thirty-four-day deadline was repealed, and the presidential electors now meet on the *second* Wednesday in December."

Speaking of date problems, New York City's David Shulman has a bone, or rather, a bagel, to pick with us. Although we mentioned in When Do Fish Sleep? *that the bagel can be traced back to Austria in 1683, Shulman, a contributor to the* Oxford English Dictionary, *cites Professor David Gold of the University of Haifa, "the best authority on the origin of the bagel," who claims that bagels were among gifts offered to pregnant women and midwives in Cracow as far back as 1610. "Gold wrote that we do not know when or where the bagel was invented. . . ."*

Reader Daniel Karlan of Waldwick, New Jersey, was passionate about another starchy argument—the difference between Italian and French breads, a topic we discussed in Aspirin:

"Your source states 'French breads . . . incorporate small amounts of shortening . . . in the formulation.' My source, the author and breadbaker Bernard Clayton, Jr., carries several different recipes for French bread in his *The Complete Book of Breads*, and the one he acquired from a French baker includes just flour, yeast, salt, and water: not even sugar is added, in complete contradiction to your source.

"I suggest that the shape, the slashing parallel to the axis, the thinness of the crust, and, as you mention, the addition of sesame seeds characterizes Italian bread and distinguishes it from true French bread. The thinness of the crust is largely due to shorter time in the oven, which also results in lighter coloring than French bread, which has a dark, glowing golden-brown thick crust—so thick its crunch as you bite into it can send chips 'flying across the room,' to quote Mr. Clayton. It is an experience not to be missed—or forgotten.

We've competed in the "flying chips for distance" contest, ourselves, Daniel. We would like to point out that except for questions about individual companies, we never rely on one source. We spoke to many bakers about this Imponderable, and frankly, we were shocked at how little consensus we found. But as an experiment, we just went to the Imponderables *Central cookbook collection and checked out French Bread recipes. The first three books we consulted all included shortening in the recipe for French bread, although only one included sugar. Typical was the recipe from Craig Claiborne's* The New York Times Cook Book, *which calls for one tablespoon of soft shortening to be added after the yeast is dissolved in water and salt, and before flour is added. Part of the problem might be that there isn't just one kind of French and Italian bread. Maybe "French bread" and "Italian bread" are as interchangeable as "French kiss" and "English kiss."*

Ultimately, we guess, it's a philosophical matter, as is Las Vegan Alan Tyler's complaint about our last sentence in the discussion of why you can't find macadamia nuts in their shells in Do Penguins Have Knees?*:*

"You state: 'Of course, one question remains. Why did Mother Nature bother creating macadamias when humans and animals (even raging rhinos) can't break open the shells to eat without the aid of machinery?'

"Obviously, the shell is there to protect the nut from being eaten. The nut is meant to grow more trees. If it were consumed, it could not do that and the species would disappear."

But really, what an empty life for a macadamia nut merely to perpetuate itself if not to be consumed by humans! And what would be served in first-class cabins on airplanes?

How about M&M's? That would be fine with Tom Marous of Chesterland, Ohio, who has used the scientific method to delve further into the "M's" in M&M candy, a topic we discussed in Why Do Clocks Run Clockwise?*:*

𝔇avid 𝔉eldman

"In the fifth grade, my science class did an experiment on what the 'M' was. We dropped an M&M (red works best) into a glass of water. We left it in the glass for about five minutes, and when we looked in the glass, the 'M' had floated to the top. Our science teacher told us that the 'M' was made of wax and sure enough, it was!"

Another food Imponderable from Clockwise *motivated Ursula Whitcher of West Linn, Oregon, to write. She has another take on why doughnut shop employees pick up the pastries you order with a piece of wax paper, and then stuff the contaminated paper back into your bag:*

"The reason they use the waxed paper to pick up the dough-nuts is so that *their hands* won't get sticky and covered with ic-ing. . . . It actually does serve a sanitary purpose, since fingers covered with icing will eventually be licked."

Why have we suddenly lost our appetite?

Perhaps it's the gentle reprimand we received from Sheri Radford, argu-ing that we didn't make a strong enough case for giving cash tips to waiters and waitresses (in How Does Aspirin Find a Headache?, *we detailed how easy it is for restaurateurs to pay the waitstaff the tips put on credit-card purchases):*

"Please don't think that a waiter or waitress will always get a tip on a credit card. I know of quite a few restaurants that dishon-estly keep any tips that are on credit cards. This practice is most prevalent in restaurants where the waitstaff do not carry their own cash and floats, but instead use one central cash reg-ister.

"It's always best to hand a tip, in cash, directly to the wait-person; otherwise, the establishment, another staff member, or even another patron might steal it. As a former waitress with lots of friends who have also waited tables, I know how frus-trating it is to lose a hard-earned tip."

In Do Penguins Have Knees?, *we speculated about the origins of why armies start marching on the left foot. Dale Neiburg of Laurel, Maryland, found a source dating back to 1589 that explored this issue:*

"As far as I know, the question was first addressed by Thoinot Arbeau in his *Orchesography:*

"'. . . [A]ssuming most soldiers to be right footed they march with the left foot first. If any of them were to start with the right and finish with the left foot they would knock shoulders when in close formation and hinder one another, because we turn the shoulder slightly to the side of the foot that is leading. . . . That is why the drummer beats a succession of repetitions of the rhythm, so that if confusion should occur . . . , the soldiers can mend matters and easily get back on the left foot when they hear the pause . . .'

"Actually, Arbeau tells us he's going to answer the question about beginning on the left foot specifically, but as far as I can see, Arbeau only explains why all soldiers should begin with the same foot, whichever that is."

And speaking of military matters, we heard from a farflung correspondent, Chris Braun of Westervoort, the Netherlands. He read our discussion of "What sadist invented the necktie? And what supposed function did it serve?" in Why Do Dogs Have Wet Noses?:

"Your explanation is quite different from the one that I learned as a child, and much less romantic. During one of the Anglo-French wars in the Middle Ages, the English beleaguered the French city of Calais. When the city wanted to surrender, the English commander insisted on a condition that a number of the most important citizens come to his camp, well prepared for their hanging. They had to be dressed in burial gowns with a noose around their necks!

"Much later, the famous French sculptor Rodin made a world-famous statue of the volunteers. Now, I don't know whether these men swung in the end or not, but from then on the French, in honor of their brave self-sacrifice, wear their scarves done up like a noose—and so does the rest of the world, dictated by fashion. (A nice addition: the Dutch word for 'tie,' *stropdas,* literally means 'noose-scarf').

"So, according to this story, we are wearing a sign of surrender and subservience—to our wives, our bosses, or just to convention."

It seems to us that the best way to honor these martyrs is by not wearing nooses around our necks, but maybe we're just bitter.

But we couldn't possibly be as bitter as reader Ivan L. Pfalser of Caney, Kansas, who, to put it mildly, disagrees with our discussion about the emergence of round haystacks in Poodles*:*

"Hay (that's a joke, son!) Buster! It's very evident that you nor your sources ever laid foot on a farm or hardly even know what one is if you drove by one.

"First of all, a word of advice: Don't ever, ever, go to a president of some hifalutin' feed company or a government agriculture representative to get a farm question answered. 99 and 44/100 percent of them are city bred and look learned and don't zap about the real world of farming or ranching. Drive out in the country and find a real farmer and if you act half-knowledgeable he will give a straight answer."

Pfalser speculates that ancient farmers probably started with roundish haystacks but larger farms in modern times needed to stack greater amounts of hay. Rectangles stack much more easily than circles—that's why building blocks are rectangular instead of circular. Furthermore, the advent of the hay baler made the haystack nearly obsolete:

"The only place today that I know of where round haystacks can be found is on *small* farm acreage where it's impractical to bring a baler in or in Amish or Mennonite communities that still farm the 'old way.' "

After a four-page dissertation on the cultural history of hay, Ivan concludes:

"Now you know almost as much about haystacks as I do, except you never had the experience of making one on a 105 degree Fahrenheit summer day with hardly a breeze blowing."

We wouldn't go near a haystack, Ivan, even to find a needle. Or a missing sock, for that matter. But Jenny Riley, of Satellite Beach, Florida, needn't bother:

"Last summer, my washing machine was working normally with no problems at all. I was getting ready to bleach a load of clothes, so I started the washer with bleach but no clothes. While I was waiting for the water to rise to capacity, suddenly three socks came flying out with the water that was filling the machine. It scared me to death.

"The worst part was that none of these socks matched any other in the house!"

Want to describe them, Jenny? There are a few hundred thousand Imponderables *readers who might match with your three flying socks.*

It's always fun to follow up and find new answers to old Imponderables. It gives us a feeling of accomplishment. Although not as great a feeling as it seems to provide for Craig Kirkland of Greenville, North Carolina, who right about now seems to feel very, very high:

"It appears that for once I can help you out! Now, I fully expect this startling, earth-shattering info to appear in your Letters section, or I'll threaten you with several dozen air-mailed fruitcakes! (Incidentally, all those letters from people professing to like that stuff are obviously some sort of elaborate prank being played on you and all your readers. I personally refuse to believe any human could survive the digestion of a single piece).

"Anyway, back in *Poodles*, you answered the question about the indentation above the upper lip known as the philtrum. The eminent William P. Jollie says that this useless body part is named for 'the Greek word *philter*, which even in English means "love potion." ' He then admits, 'I confess I don't see a connection . . .'

"Ha! Ha! Ha! If either of you were as brilliant as I am and just happened to be reading *2201 Fascinating Facts* by David Louis about five years ago and remembered a place to look in said book after reading *Poodles,* then you would have come up with a very impressive quote to let the world know how this name came about. From page 222:

" 'The indentation in the middle of the area between the nose and upper lip has a name. It is called the philtrum . . . Among the ancient Greeks this innocent little dent was considered one of the body's most erogenous zones.'

"See? 'Love potion.' 'Philter.' 'Erogenous zone.' I bet you're *thrilled* with my deductive powers."

You've discovered that a part of the body long considered useless is actually the "P-Spot," the key to our sensual pleasure. Craig, we're overwhelmed. We can't go on.

So we'll wish all of our readers a happy and healthy year. While we go off and rub every single philtrum we can find.

Acknowledgments

❧ As always, my first and most important acknowledgment is to you. All authors with a semblance of sanity appreciate their readers. But I owe a special debt to you, for your letters create the Imponderables, solve the Frustables, and provide the inspiration when we consider ditching the writing gig and pursuing an easier profession, like coal mining.

As usual, we fell behind in answering correspondence over the past year, and we can't promise we will be speedier this year. But I can assure you that I value and read personally every letter received at *Imponderables*. If you send a self-addressed stamped envelope, you will get a personal reply. And if you send an E-mail, chances are you'll receive an even quicker reply.

You may have noticed that *Imponderables* has a new home. I'm happy to be at Putnam and even happier for the opportunity to work with Neil Nyren, who was actually a fan of this dubious enterprise before he became my editor. And I was lucky, indeed, that his son, Alex, sparked Neil's interest. As this is being written, I haven't met most of the other folks at Putnam who will be toiling on my behalf, but I would like to mention two terrific people I have: my publicist, Judy Burns; and Neil's assistant, Michele Fiegoli.

My professional relationship with my agent, Jim Trupin, has lasted for ten books and ten years, longer than the Beatles and Brian Epstein or George Steinbrenner and Billy Martin. We're grizzled veterans now, when we once were merely grizzled. We still haven't been together as long as Shari Lewis and Lamb Chop, or Manny, Moe, and Jack, but we're happily working on it. And thanks to the ungrizzled Liz Trupin for her support over the years.

Kassie Schwan has illustrated all ten books, much to my pleasure. Several readers have asked who comes up with the ideas for her drawings. The simple answer: Kassie.

For their invaluable research, thanks to Dara Curran, Phil Feldman, and Sherry Spitzer.

Gratitude aplenty to my friends and family, who have abided my whining with good humor (or at least, resignation). We're not going to include the laundry list of friends we have in the past, if only because by its size it was beginning to resemble a list of Madonna's paramours. So here are the friends and family who have lent ears most often when we bounced around ideas about our work over the past two years: Fred Feldman; Phil Feldman; Gilda Feldman; Michael Feldman; Michele Gallery; Michael Barson; Uday Ivatury; Laura Tolkow; Christal Henner; Roy Welland; Ju-

dith Dahlman; Paul Dahlman; Bonnie Gellas; James Gleick; Chris Mc-
Cann; Amy Glass; Judy Goulding; Mark Kohut; Karen Stoddard; Joanna
Parker; Brian Rose; Susan DiSesa; Steve Monaco; Elizabeth Frenchman;
Ken Gordon; Merrill Perlman; Harvey Kleinman; Stewart Kellerman; Pat
O'Conner; Terry Johnson; Maggie Wittenburg; Susie Russenberger; Larry
Prussin; Jon Blees; and the ever-loving, frog-spitting Housewife Writers.

And many thanks to the staff of Starbucks 809, for keeping me vertical.

My experience at HarperCollins was a wonderful one. Although there
is not room to list all of the terrific people who were cherished partners
and friends, I would like to acknowledge some of the most important: Rick
Kot; Bill Shinker; Sheila Gilooly; Mark Landau; Connie Levinson; Barbara
Rittenhouse; Joan Urban; Diane Burrowes; Virginia Stanley; Sean Dugan;
Brenda Marsh; Craig Herman; Wende Gozan; Allison Pennels; Karen
Mender; Steve Magnuson; Roz Barrow; and Susan Friedland.

In preparation for this book, we contacted more than 1,000 experts—
professors, corporate executives, sports officials, choreographers, and
coroners. One of the greatest joys of our work is learning about subjects
we know nothing about from the top experts in their fields. Without their
generosity, all Imponderables would turn out to be Frustables. The following were sources who led directly to answers in this book:

Beth Adams, H.J. Heinz Company; N. B. Albert, Florsheim Company;
Alumax Foils, Inc.; American Academy of Dermatology; Lynn Anderson,
Borden, Inc.; Jerome Andrews; Jerry Aronow.

Paul Bagley; Jan Balkin, American Trucking Assn.; Joshua Bardwell;
Joseph P. Bark; Kathryn Bayne, National Institutes of Health; Lynn Bee-
dle, Council on Tall Buildings and Urban Habitat; Rich Beerman; Ben
Benjamin, Good Humor–Breyers Ice Cream; Stewart Berg; Denis
Bergquist; Don Berkowitz; Stan Berry; Biff Bilstein, Neodata Services;
Ronald Blankers, See's Candies; Mark Blythe, Fender Musical Instru-
ments; Debbie Bolding, 9-Lives/Star-Kist Foods; E.T. Bond, Kimberly-
Clark Corporation; Barry Bowen, Tootsie Roll Industries; G. Bruce Boyer;
Frank Brennan, United States Postal Service; Merrill Brown, Crane Busi-
ness Papers; Tom Brown; Dennis Buege; Thomas Burns, American Spice
Trade Assn.; Thomas Busey, Bureau of Alcohol, Tobacco and Firearms; Jay
Butler; Trish Butler, Social Security Administration; Robert Byrne, Inter-
national Ice Cream Assn.

Lucio Caputo, Italian Wine and Food Inst.; Glenn Carriker, Alliance
for Traffic Safety; Bob Carroll, Pro Football Researchers Assn.; Lloyd
Casey, U.S. Forest Service; John Clark, Social Security Administration;
Clorox Company; Frank Coburn, Abraham Lincoln Museum; Ron Cohen; Roger Coleman, National Food Processors Assn.; John Conroy, Core-
craft Industry; Kenneth L. Coskey, Navy Historical Foundation; Larry

Costello, University of California Cooperative Extension; Chris Cowles, Otis Elevator; James Cramer, American Institute of Architects; Terry Cummerford, Natick Research and Development Center; Fred Cunningham, City of Beverly Hills Public Affairs.

Jack Daniel's Distillery; Lorraine D'Antonio, Religious Research Assn.; Donald Davidson, United States Auto Club; Michael De Marco; Lance Deckinger, National Baseball Congress; Al Decoteau, Society of Parrot Breeders and Exhibitors; Pauline Delli-Carpini, International Linen Promotion Commission; Mr. Demma, U.S. Army Center of Military History; Democratic National Committee; Andrew DeWeerd; Diane Dickey, Kellogg Company; Dale Diebold, Leathercraft Guild; Anne Diestel, U.S. Department of Justice; Tim Dillon, Cornell Laboratory of Ornithology; Kadir Donmez, American Leather Chemists Assn.; Paul Droste, North American Brass Band Assn.

Jonathan Egre; Tom Elliott, Canned Fruit Promotion Service; Robert Ermatinger, Luggage and Leather Goods Manufacturers; Todd Lee Etzel, Jim Evans, Jim Evans Academy of Professional Umpiring.

J. F. Farrington, National Assn. of Scissors and Shears Manufacturers; Rob Farson, Neodata Services; Betty Feagans, Royal China and Porcelain Companies; Clinton Fields, Friends of the National Zoo; Martha Fischer, Cornell Laboratory of Ornithology; Donna Florio, Pfizer, Inc.; David Fowler; Laurence Frank, Berkeley Project; Harry Frost, Dyson-Perrins Museum.

Brendan Gaffney, Pepsi-Cola; Samuel R. Gammon, American Historical Assn.; George Gantner, National Assn. of Medical Examiners; Genovese Drug Stores; Larry Gerlach; Alan Gettlemen, Bobrick Washroom Equipment; Mary Gillespie, Assn. of Home Appliances Manufacturers; Gerald Gladstone; Jeff Glenning, Reynolds Metals Company; Todd Glickman, American Meteorological Society; Louis Gomberg, Academy of Master Wine Growers; Michael Graham, St. Louis University Medical Center; George L. Graveson, Naval Submarine League; Helen Grayson, American Restaurant China Council; Alvin Grobmeier.

Tracy Haak, Assn. of Home Appliance Manufacturers; Richard Hambleton; Bill Hamilton; Tom Hammill, *Referee* magazine; Ed Hansen, American Assn. of Zoo Keepers; Sandra Harding, United States Postal Service; Barb Harris, The Standing Partnership; David Henning, University of Iowa; David J. Hensing, Assn. of American Highway Safety and Traffic Officials; Jeff Herman, Society of American Silversmiths; Jack Herschlag, National Assn. of Men's Sportswear Buyers; Gregory Higby, American Inst. of the History of Pharmacy; Robert Hill, Internal Revenue Service; Ruth Hill, Internal Revenue Service; Myron Hinrichs, Hasti Friends of the Elephant; Mark Holland, National Tabletop Assn.; Marsha Holloman, American Pharmaceutical Assn.; Derek Holstein, Guernoc Winery Estates

Vineyard; Tom Horan, American Irish Historical Society; John Horvath, United Transportation Union; J. Benjamin Horvay; Richard Hudnut, Builders Hardware Manufacturers Assn.; Rebecca Hutton, National Dance Assn.

Mark Incley; Janet Ivaldi, Pepsico.

Simon S. Jackel; Chris Jones, Pepsi-Cola.

Marlene Kahan, American Society of Magazine Editors; Naomi Kaminsky, American Pharmaceutical Assn.; Glenda Karrenbrock, Tandy Leather Company; John Kendall, Otis Elevator Company; Connie M. Kent, Miles Laboratories; John Kepplinger, Kellogg Company; Bruce Kershner; Wayne O. Kester, American Assn. of Equine Practitioners; Dusty Kidd, Nike Inc.; Linda Kilbryde, World Dryer Corporation; Thomas P. Krugman, California Cling Peach Advisory Board; Bill Kruidenier, International Society of Aboriculture; Ken Kunkel, American Assn. of State Climatologists.

John Lanctot, DePaul University; Herbert Lapidus, Combe, Inc.; Michael Lauria; Bob Laycock, Indianapolis Motor Speedway; Leaf, Inc.; Judy Lederich, Friskies PetCare Company; Margot Lehman, American Dance Guild; Thomas A. Lehmann, American Institute of Baking; Lowell Levine, New York State Police Forensics Science Unit; Abraham Lincoln Assn.; Jerome Z. Litt; Chuck Loebbaka, Northwestern University; Susan Lumpkin, Friends of the National Zoo; Theodore Lustig, West Virginia University; John Lutley, Gold Inst.

Deb Magness, Heinz U.S.A.; Gregg Manuel, California Highway Patrol; Ed Marks; Anthony Martin, National Flag Foundation; Susan Mauro, Pepsi-Cola; Mary Anne Mayeski, College Theology Society; Lori McManes, Coca-Cola USA; Art McNally, National Football League; Teresa McNally, Burger King Corporation; Paul Meehan; Myrna Metzger, American Dairy Assn. of Indiana; Anthony Meushaw, Society of Soft Drink Technologists; Jeff Milder, Spaulding Sports Worldwide; John Miller; Randy Morgan, Cincinnati Insectarium; John Moynihan, Shoe Trades Publishing Company; Polly Murphy, McCormick & Company; Charles Myers, Leather Industries of America.

Rick Nedderman; Nestlé Foods Corporation; Newspaper Assn. of America; Samuel Nichols, Quality Chekd Dairy Products Assn.; Doris Nixon, National Bridal Service; Joe Nucci, Mann Packing Company.

Robert O'Brien, National Safety Council; Bill O'Connor, Topps Chewing Gum; Office of Vehicle Research.

Bob Park, American Physical Society; Connie Parker, National Assn. of Institutional Linen Management; John Payton; Carmi Penny, San Diego Zoo; Jed Peretz; Geoff Phelps, Spalding Sports Worldwide; James Plumb, Aluminum Assn. Library; Elsa Posey; Bruce Powell, Otis Elevator Company; Steven Price; Henry Printz, Associated Locksmiths of America; Judy Provo, Purdue University.

Qantas Airways Ltd.

Howard Raether; George W. Rambo, National Pest Control Assn.; Mel Rapp, Quality Chekd Dairy Products Assn.; Jan Razek, Revco Drug Stores; Joe Reed; Erroll Rhodes, American Bible Society; John R. Rodenburg, Federated Funeral Directors of America; Nalini Rogers, Federal Reserve Board; William A. Rossi, William A. Rossi Associates; Linda Rozell, New York Department of Motor Vehicles; Ian Russell.

Bob Sanders, University of California, Berkeley; Leslie Saul-Gershenz, San Francisco Zoological Society; Denise Schippers, Maytag Corporation; Doreen Schmidt, Consortium of Chianti Classico; Ray Schmidt; Jennifer Schmits, Indianapolis Project, Inc.; Steven Schutz, University of California, Berkeley Mosquito Control Laboratory; Heidi Schwartz, *Today's Facility Manager;* Henry Schwarzchild, National Coalition to Abolish the Death Penalty; Barbara Selby, NASA; Samuel Selden; John Shaw, American Helicopter Society; Tim Shelfer; Barbara Singer, Footwear Industries of America; Whitney Smith, Flag Research Center; Al Snapper; Tim Socha, Rawlings Sporting Goods; Ronald Sohn, Shoe Service Inst. of America; Philip Sorensen, Advanced Technology Innovations; Michael Spates, United States Postal Service; Shirley Starke, Irish SIG of Mensa; Bill Steele, Rawlings Sporting Goods; Ernie Stephens, Werewolf Aviation; John Stephens; Stan Sterenberg; Judy Stern, Noritake Company; Lisa Stevens, National Zoo; Cheryl Stewart-Miller, Heinz U.S.A.; Dave Stidholf, Mann Packing Company; David Stivers, Nabisco; Brett Stone, Russell Stover; Melvin Stromberg, World Assn. of Veterinary Anatomists.

Stephen Teter; Kristin Thelander, University of Iowa; R. D. Thompson, Teledyne Engineering; Ben Thorp, James River Corporation; Drew Todd, Ohio Dept. of Natural Resources; Trans World Airlines, Inc.; Brian Traynor, National Highway Traffic and Safety Administration; Allen Tyson, Diebold, Inc.

Gene Ulm, Republican National Committee; University of Miami; University of North Carolina.

Chuck Vanstrom, Neodata Services; Tony Verlezza, Good Humor–Breyers.

James Watt; Marcia Watt, Arts of the Book Collection, Sterling Memorial Library; Elsie Diven Weigel, NASA; Robert Weiss, United States Postal Service; Mike White, Bureau of the Mint; John Whooley, Irish American Foundation; Dale Williams; Janet Collins Williams, American Meat Inst.; Mary Ellen Withrow, Treasurer of the United States; Chris Woodruff, Massachusetts Department of Motor Vehicles.

Gang Xu, Jefferson University.

Karen Yoder, Entomological Society of America; George York, University of California, Davis; Laura Young, Heinz Pet Products; W. F. Young, Inc.; John Yurkus, Home Baking Assn.

Robert J. Zedik, National Confectioners Assn. of the U.S.; Jeffrey Zelkowitz, United States Postal Service.

And our special thanks to the many sources who helped us with the answers in the book but preferred to remain anonymous.

Index

HELP!

Folks have been telling us for the longest time that we need help. OK, we'll admit it.

We need new Imponderables. We need your Frustables solutions. And your letters of praise, amplification, or even expressions of rancor.

We may be needy, but we come bearing gifts. If you are the first to pose an Imponderable we use, or offer the best solution to one of our ten new Frustables, you'll receive a complimentary copy of your contribution, along with an acknowledgment in the book.

If you would like a personal response, please send a self-addressed stamped envelope (no need for a SASE if you don't need a reply—all correspondence is welcome). Please be patient—at times it takes us much longer to reply than we would like.

Mail your "help" along with your name, address, and (optional) phone number to:

IMPONDERABLES
P.O. Box 24815
Los Angeles, California 90024

And we're happy to announce that *Imponderables* has invaded cyberspace. Instead of a letter, why not try E-mailing us through the Internet or Prodigy? Chances are, we will be able to reply quicker via E-mail than through "snail mail." Please include your full name and mailing address, though.

INTERNET: "feldman@imponderables.com"
PRODIGY: "BNBR03A"

Or join us at the Imponderables home page on the World Wide Web:

"http: // WWW. imponderables. com"

Special Call to Imponderables Readers:

❦ We're happy to announce that we are diving into our project of writing an entire volume devoted to unraveling the ultimate mystery: What's the deal with the opposite sex?

Perhaps we are foolish to delve into these murky waters that have drowned wiser folks than us. But we have a secret weapon: you. You can help us in two ways:

1. Write to us about what mystifies you, peeves you, irritates you, frustrates you, or baffles you about anything regarding the opposite sex (its beliefs, customs, anatomy, rituals, habits, psychology, and bizarre preferences are all fair game).

2. If you'd be willing to represent your gender, let us know. We'll send you a questionnaire that will give you the opportunity to reveal to members of the opposite sex the *ultimate truth* that they have been craving. Men and women, boys and girls of any age and background are welcome.

As always, you can reach us at *Imponderables* Central:

IMPONDERABLES
P.O. Box 24815
Los Angeles, California 90024

INTERNET: "feldman@imponderables.com"
PRODIGY: "BNBR03A"